THE
BEST
AMERICAN
POETRY
2009

◇ ◇ ◇

David Wagoner, Editor

David Lehman, Series Editor

SCRIBNER POETRY

NEW YORK   LONDON   TORONTO   SYDNEY

SCRIBNER POETRY
A Division of Simon & Schuster, Inc.
1230 Avenue of the Americas
New York, NY 10020

Copyright © 2009 by David Lehman
Foreword copyright © 2009 by David Lehman
Introduction copyright © 2009 by David Wagoner

First Scribner edition September 2009

SCRIBNER and design are registered trademarks of The Gale Group, Inc.,
used under license by Simon & Schuster, Inc., the publisher of this work.

For information about special discounts for bulk purchases,
please contact Simon & Schuster Special Sales at 1-866-506-1949
or business@simonandschuster.com.

The Simon & Schuster Speakers Bureau can bring authors to your live event.
For more information or to book an event contact the Simon & Schuster Speakers
Bureau at 1-866-248-3049 or visit our website at www.simonspeakers.com.

Manufactured in the United States of America

1 3 5 7 9 10 8 6 4 2

Library of Congress Control Number: 88644281

ISBN 978-0-7432-9976-3
ISBN 978-0-7432-9977-0 (pbk)
ISBN 978-1-4391-6626-0 (ebook)

CONTENTS

David Lehman was born in New York City in 1948. His books of poetry include *Yeshiva Boys* (2009), *When a Woman Loves a Man* (2005), *The Evening Sun* (2002), and *The Daily Mirror* (2000), all from Scribner. Lehman has edited *The Oxford Book of American Poetry* (Oxford University Press, 2006), *The Best American Erotic Poems* (Scribner, 2008), and *Great American Prose Poems* (Scribner, 2003), among other collections. He has written six nonfiction books, most recently *A Fine Romance: Jewish Songwriters, American Songs* (Nextbook, 2009). He has received fellowships from the Guggenheim Foundation and the National Endowment for the Arts as well as the Award in Literature from the American Academy of Arts and Letters. He has taught in the graduate writing program of the New School in New York City since the program's inception in 1996. He initiated *The Best American Poetry* series in 1988. He lives in New York City.

FOREWORD

by David Lehman

⬦   ⬦   ⬦

What is a poet? In his "Defense of Poetry," Shelley writes, "A poet is a nightingale, who sits in darkness and sings to cheer its own solitude with sweet sounds; his auditors are as men entranced by the melody of an unseen musician, who feel that they are moved and softened, yet know not whence or why." The solitude and sweet darkness, the emphasis on the unseen, the nightingale as the image of the poet, the listeners entranced but bewildered: how romantic this formulation is—and how well it fits its author. Matthew Arnold alters the metaphor but retains something of its tone when he calls Shelley "a beautiful and ineffectual angel, beating in the void his luminous wings in vain." Kierkegaard in *Either/Or* goes further than either Shelley or Arnold in accentuating the negative. In a passage I've long admired, Kierkegaard identifies the poet as one whose heart is full of anguish but whose lips transform all sighs and groans into beautiful music. Kierkegaard likens the fate of this "unhappy" individual to the cruel and unusual punishment meted out by the tyrant Phalaris, whose unfortunate victims, "slowly roasted by a gentle fire" in a huge copper bull, let out shrieks that turn into sweet melodies by the time they reach the tyrant's ears. The success of the poet, then, corresponds to the amount of agony endured. Readers clamor for more, for they are aware only of the music and not of the suffering that went into it. The critics, too, stand ready to applaud—if, that is, the poet's work meets the requirements of the immutable "laws of aesthetics." And here Kierkegaard's parable acquires an extra layer of irony, the better to convey his contempt for critics. "Why, to be sure," he writes, "a critic resembles a poet as one pea another, the only difference being that he has no anguish in his heart and no music on his lips." And therefore, Kierkegaard concludes with a flourish, sooner would he be a swineherd understood by the swine than a poet misunderstood by men.

Kierkegaard's argument proceeds by the logic of his similes—the sweet music, the barbaric torture, the prosaic peas in the pod, the swineherd as an honorable profession—and the abrupt tonal shift at the end from sarcasm to defiance. If, as Wallace Stevens asserted, "poetry is almost incredibly one of the effects of analogy," here is a gorgeous example. The passage has the virtue, moreover, of raising questions about the occupational hazards that poets face and about their relation to a world of readers and reviewers.

In one way, at least, Kierkegaard's parable is untrue to the experience of American poets, who rarely have to fend off legions of avid admirers. But the notion that the job of the critic is to find fault with the poetry— that the aims of criticism and of poetry are opposed—is still with us or, rather, has returned after a hiatus. It was once erroneously thought that devastating reviews caused John Keats's untimely death in his twenty-sixth year. Lord Byron in *Don Juan* had Keats and his reviewers in mind when he wrote, "'Tis strange the mind, that very fiery particle, / Should let itself be snuff'd out by an article." In reality, however, it was not criticism but consumption that cut short Keats's life.[1] Many of us delight in Oscar Wilde's witty paradoxes that blur the identities of artist and critic.[2] The critical essays of T. S. Eliot and W. H. Auden are continuous with their poems and teach us that criticism is a matter not of enforcing the "laws of aesthetics" or meting out sentences as a judge might pronounce them in court. Rather, the poet as critic engages with works of literature and enriches our understanding and enjoyment of them. Yet today more than a few commentators seem intent on punishing the authors they review. It has grown into a phenomenon. In the March 2009 issue of *Poetry,* the critic Jason Guriel defends "negativity" as "the poetry review-er's natural posture, the default position she assumes before scanning a single line." The title of Guriel's piece sums it up: "Going Negative."

The romantic image of the poet as a vulnerable personage in a hos-tile universe has not gone out of currency. The poet is doomed to go unrecognized and to pay dearly for his music-making powers. The gift of poetry comes not as an unalloyed blessing but as the incidental virtue

---

1. Not that the critics were blameless. The anonymous reviewer writing for *Blackwood's Edinburgh Magazine* (August 1818) called Keats's *Endymion* "imper-turbable driveling idiocy." Endymion was supposed to be "a Greek shepherd loved by a Grecian goddess," but in Keats's hands, he was "merely a young Cockney rhymester."

2. In *The Critic as Artist,* Wilde radically revises Matthew Arnold on the func-tion of criticism. According to Arnold, the endeavor is "to see the object as in itself it really is." According to Wilde, the aim is "to see the object as in itself it really is not."

of a defect or as compensation for a loss, an injury, an ailment, a deficiency. Edmund Wilson coined the phrase that readily comes to mind for this dynamic of compensatory balance: "the wound and the bow." Before it served Wilson as the title of a collection of his essays (1941), the phrase headed his study of the myth of Philoctetes, which the critic took as paradigmatic of the artist's situation. Aeschylus, Euripides, and Sophocles treated the myth in plays; the *Philoctetes* of Sophocles survives. The hero, who excels even Odysseus at archery, possesses the invincible bow that once belonged to Hercules. Philoctetes joins the Greeks in their assault on Troy but is bitten by a poisonous snake, and the suppurating wound emits so foul an odor that his comrades-in-arms abandon him on the island of Lemnos. There he is stranded for ten miserable years. But when a Trojan prophet is forced to reveal that the Greeks will fail to conquer Troy without the unerring bow of Philoctetes, a platoon is dispatched to reenlist the archer—who is understandably reluctant to return to the fray—and to recover his arms by any means necessary. In Sophocles, Philoctetes is cured at Troy. He goes on to kill Paris, the Trojan prince whose abduction of Helen precipitated the epic conflict, and he becomes one of the heroes of the Greek victory. One lesson, according to Wilson, is that "genius and disease, like strength and mutilation, may be inextricably bound up together." In the most speculative and provocative sentence in the essay, Wilson ventures that "somewhere even in the fortunate Sophocles there had been a sick and raving Philoctetes."

W. H. Auden's early prose poem, "Letter to a Wound" (1931), is a powerful modern statement of the theme: "You are so quiet these days that I get quite nervous, remove the dressing. I am safe, you are still there." Addressing the wound as "you" is not merely a grammatical convenience but the vehicle of a linguistic transformation; the ailment becomes an active, willful muse and companion—albeit one whose traits include "insane jealousy," "bad manners," and a "passion for spoiling things." The letter writer has learned to live with his incurable condition as with a secret partner, an illicit lover. They have even gone through a "honeymoon stage" together. "Thanks to you," Auden writes, "I have come to see a profound significance in relations I never dreamt of considering before, an old lady's affection for a small boy, the Waterhouses and their retriever, the curious bond between Offal and Snig, the partners in the hardware shop in the front." The wound is not named, though we read of a visit to a surgeon, who begins a sentence, "I'm afraid," and need not add a word. The particular virtue of this epistolary prose poem is that "I" and "you," a pair of pronouns, are raised to the level of a universal duality and are therefore greater than any specific duality that seems appropriate—whether "artist" and "wound," or "self" and "soul," or "ego" and "id," or "lover" and "beloved."

It is difficult not to fall under the spell of Wilson's wound and bow or of the corresponding myth in the Hebraic tradition. In the thirty-second chapter of Genesis, Jacob—who twice in the past had got the better of his brother Esau, both times by cunning or deceit—must wrestle with "a man" who will not reveal his name and who must flee the scene at daybreak. The struggle takes place on the eve of his first encounter with Esau after many years, in the deep darkness of the night, and it is physical combat of a kind not associated with Jacob. When he fights the angel to a standstill, he receives a blessing and a new name, Israel (because he has "contended with God and men and has prevailed"). But he has also suffered a wound "in the hollow of his thigh" that causes him to limp thereafter. The story is rich and mysterious in inverse proportion to its length: nine biblical verses. Though each is said to be a source of power, the Hebrew blessing bestowed on Jacob is utterly different from the Greek bow. Yet at bottom we find the familiar dialectic of compensation.

Such myths may console us. The logic of Emerson's essay "Compensation" has saved my spirits on many a dismal afternoon. "The sure years reveal the deep emotional force that underlies all facts," Emerson writes. "The death of a dear friend, wife, brother, lover, which seemed nothing but privation, somewhat later assumes the aspect of a guide or genius; for it commonly operates revolutions in our way of life, terminates an epoch of infancy or of youth which was waiting to be closed, breaks up a wonted occupation, or a household, or style of living, and allows the formation of new ones more friendly to the growth of character." It is to Emerson's essay that I turn when I need to tamp down the impulses of resentment or envy and reconcile myself to realities. There is wisdom here and truth, a counterargument if not exactly a solution to the problem of evil that Gerard Manley Hopkins stated summarily: "Why do sinners' ways prosper? And why must / Disappointment all I endeavor end?"

There is also, however, a danger in the intimate association of genius and illness, especially mental illness, especially at a time when many of us engaged in the discourse of poetry come into contact with ever-increasing numbers of impressionable young people who want to study creative writing. The romantic conception of the poet can lead too easily to self-pity or worse, the glorification of madness and the idealization of the self-inflicted wound. We need to remember that poetry springs from joy as often as from sorrow: the impulse to praise is as strong as the impulse to mourn. Lionel Trilling's essay "Art and Neurosis" is a vital corrective to the tendency to assent too readily to propositions obscuring the differences between genius and madness. Trilling accepts the premise that all of us, including "the fortunate Sophocles," are ill; we are all neurotic. In that case, it is not the primal hurt but the ability to rise above it that distinguishes the artist. Poetry is not a matter of divine madness but the product of labor and conscious mind. "Nothing is so characteristic of the artist as his power of shaping his work, of subjugating his raw material, however aberrant it be from what we call normality," Trilling writes. "What marks the artist is his power to shape the material of pain we all have."

My favorite sentence in Kierkegaard's parable is the one in which poets and critics are considered identical except that the latter lack the very qualities—the anguish in the heart and the music on the lips—that are definitive of the poet. For many years I resisted Kierkegaard's "either/ or" logic. I felt that there needn't be a structural enmity between poetry and criticism. Now I wonder.

The characteristic badness of literary criticism in the 1980s was that it was heavily driven by theory and saddled with an unlovely vocabulary. T. S. Eliot, in "The Function of Criticism" (1923), says he "presumes" that "no exponent of criticism" has "ever made the preposterous assumption that criticism is an autotelic activity"—that is, an activity to be undertaken as an end in itself without connection to a work of literature. Eliot did not figure on post-structuralism and the critic's declaration of independence from the text. If you wanted criticism "constantly to be confronted with examples of poetry," as R. P. Blackmur recommends in "A Critic's Job of Work," you were in for a bad time in the 1980s. The academic critics' disregard of contemporary poetry paralleled the rise of creative writing as a field of study and, partly in consequence, the writing of poetry did not suffer, though from time to time you would hear the tired refrain that poetry—like God, the novel as a form, and the author altogether—had died. This shibboleth itself has not perished. *Newsweek* reports that, despite "anecdotal evidence that interest in poetry is on the rise," statistics show a decline. "Is an art form dying?" the magazine asks.[3] Donald Hall wrote the definitive response to these premature death notices, "Death to the Death of

3. Marc Bain, "The End of Verse?" *Newsweek,* March 25, 2009.

Poetry," which served as the introduction to *The Best American Poetry 1989*. Hall's assertion remains valid: "American poetry survives; it even prevails."

Poetry criticism at its worst today is mean in spirit and spiteful in intent, as if determined to inflict the wound that will spur the artist to new heights if it does not cripple him or her. Somewhere along the line, the notion took hold that poets were reluctant to write honestly about their peers. But in the absence of critics who are not themselves poets, surely the antidote is not to encourage the habit of rejection without explanation, denunciation without a reasoned argument, and a slam of the gavel in high dudgeon as if a poem were a felony. Hostile criticism, criticism by insult, may have entertainment value, but animus does not guarantee honesty. As one who knows from firsthand experience what a book reviewer faces when writing on deadline, I can tell the real thing when I see it, and the hysterical over-the-top attack is as often as not the product of a pose. Every critic knows it is easier (and more fun) to write a ruthless review rather than a measured one. As a reviewer, you're not human if you don't give vent to your outrage once or twice—if only to get the impulse out of you. If you have too good a time writing hostile reviews, you'll injure not only your sensibility but your soul. Frank O'Hara felt he had no responsibility to respond to a bad poem. It'll "slip into oblivion without my help," he would say.

William Logan typifies the bilious reviewer of our day. He has attacked, viciously, a great many American poets; I, too, have been the object of his scorn. Logan is the critic as O'Hara defined the species: "the assassin of my orchards." You can rely on him to go for the most wounding gesture. Michael Palmer writes a "Baudelaire Series" of poems, for example, and Logan comments, "Baudelaire would have eaten Mr. Palmer for breakfast, with salt." The poems of Australian poet Les Murray seem "badly translated out of Old Church Slavonic with only a Russian phrase book at hand." Reviewing a book by Adrienne Rich is a task that Logan feels he could almost undertake in his sleep. Reading C. K. Williams is "like watching a dog eat its own vomit."

For many years, Logan reserved his barbs for the poets of our time. More recently he has sneered at Emily Dickinson ("a bloodless recluse") and condescended to Emerson ("a mediocre poet"). And still the *New York Times Book Review* turned to Logan to review the new edition of Frank O'Hara's *Selected Poems* last summer. Logan's piece began with the observation that O'Hara's death at the age of forty in a freak accident was a "good career move." This is not a particularly original phrase, but in O'Hara's case it is doubly unkind, giving the false impression that he died by his own hand.

Logan's treatment of Langdon Hammer's Library of America edition of Hart Crane's poetry and prose—which ran in the *New York Times Book Review* in January 2007—provoked among many readers the feeling that here he had gone too far. The piece dwelled on Crane's "sexual appetites," which "were voracious and involved far too many sailors," and included a flip dismissal of Crane's poem "Chaplinesque" (a "dreadful mess"). The review triggered off a spate of letters that the *Times* duly printed. Rosanna Warren summed up what many felt: "Snide biographical snippets about homosexuality and alcoholism are not literary criticism, nor are poems illuminated by sarcastic bons mots ('a Myth of America conceived by Tiffany and executed by Disney,' 'like being stuck in a mawkish medley from *Show Boat* and *Oklahoma!*'). Crane's revelatory weaknesses as well as his, yes, genius, deserved a more responsible accounting."

Wounded by the outcry, Logan wrote a lengthy defense of himself and his procedures in the October 2008 issue of *Poetry*. More letters to the editor followed: three pages of them in the December 2008 issue, along with a concluding comment by Logan longer than the combined efforts of the correspondents. For one who routinely seeks to give offense, Logan turns out to be thin-skinned. In the end he falls back on the argument that it is fruitless to argue in matters of taste. "The problem with taste is, yours is right and everyone else's is wrong," Logan writes. Bosh. The real problem is that Logan confuses taste with bias. Using the Romantic poets as an example, he writes: "You can't stand that ditherer Coleridge, she can't stand that whiner Keats, I can't stand that dry fussbudget Wordsworth, and we all hate Shelley." Only someone for whom poets are merely names, abstractions that never had a flesh-and-blood existence, could so gleefully reduce these poets to those epithets. But when Logan returns to "Chaplinesque," Hart Crane's "hapless little" poem (and how that unnecessary "little" rankles), he gives the game away.

Here is "Chaplinesque":

> We make our meek adjustments,
> Contented with such random consolations
> As the wind deposits
> In slithered and too ample pockets.

For we can still love the world, who find
A famished kitten on the step, and know
Recesses for it from the fury of the street,
Or warm torn elbow coverts.

We will sidestep, and to the final smirk
Dally the doom of that inevitable thumb
That slowly chafes its puckered index toward us,
Facing the dull squint with what innocence
And what surprise!

And yet these fine collapses are not lies
More than the pirouettes of any pliant cane;
Our obsequies are, in a way, no enterprise.
We can evade you, and all else but the heart:
What blame to us if the heart live on.

The game enforces smirks; but we have seen
The moon in lonely alleys make
A grail of laughter of an empty ash can,
And through all sound of gaiety and quest
Have heard a kitten in the wilderness.

To Logan the poem's concluding lines are self-evidently "embar-
rassing," an adjective he uses twice without substantiation. In the three
separate pieces in which Logan brings up the poem, he lazily repeats
the same charges, uses the same modifiers: the penultimate stanza of
"Chaplinesque" is "hapless and tone deaf," the ending is "schmaltz,"
and the poem as a whole is evidence that the poet was "star-struck" by
Charlie Chaplin, whose movies inspired Crane.

Everyone is entitled to an opinion, but a professional critic has
the responsibility to develop opinions, not just to state them. Rather
than make the effort to see how Crane's poem works as a response to
Chaplin's film *The Kid,* Logan ridicules the "star-struck" poet, likening
Chaplin then to Angelina Jolie now, a comparison of dubious value that
manages to insult everyone including Chaplin, Crane, Angelina Jolie,
and the "seventy-seven American poets" who, Logan says in his patented
blend of self-regard and snarky wit, have written odes to Jolie because
Logan wrote that Crane met Chaplin after writing "Chaplinesque."

I do not claim to comprehend "Chaplinesque" perfectly, but I believe that the lover of poetry will recognize the genius in this poem before any irritable reaching after paraphrase. Crane's repeated use of the homonym for his first name—"We can evade you, and all else but the heart: / What blame to us if the heart live on"—seems to me, for example, well worth pondering in the context of the lines' pronomial ambiguity. The poem's opening stanzas are so rich one wants to say them over and over, to speculate on the idea of the Chaplin persona as an image of the poet, of the "famished kitten" as an image of poetry, or to contemplate the remarkable sequence of "smirk," "thumb," and "squint" in the third stanza. The finger-in-the-eye slapstick comedy routine has never seemed so threatening, even if we can "Dally the doom of that inevitable thumb / That slowly chafes its puckered index toward us." The poem's ending is particularly memorable. You may not make easy sense of that "grail of laughter" created by the moon out of a garbage can in a deserted alley. But this arresting image that fuses the sacred and the profane, sky and slum, will not soon depart from your consciousness. The key phrase here, "a grail of laughter," is a great example of a poetic image that defies logical analysis, for we instinctively grasp it as a figure of the sublime, though we know that a grail cannot be "of" laughter in any conventional sense. The laughter is the "sound of gaiety and quest," and "we" can see the miracle, behold the grail, because we have heard the cry of the alley cat, and we know that poetry is not simply a grand visionary quest but also something very precious and vulnerable, a kitten in the wilderness.

The critic whose take on "Chaplinesque" I'd like to see is Christopher Ricks. Ricks begins his book *T. S. Eliot and Prejudice* with a reading of the most audacious poetic debut of the twentieth century. You might have thought that "The Love Song of J. Alfred Prufrock" would require the critic to digress from a consideration of prejudice, the focal point of Ricks's study of Eliot. Not so. Ricks quotes the uncanny stand-alone couplet that Eliot uses twice: "In the room the women come and go / Talking of Michelangelo." What have scholars said about the lines? The Oxford don Helen Gardner hears "high-pitched feminine voices" that are absurdly inadequate to the "giant art" of Michelangelo. Grover Smith says he has "no doubt" the women are talking "tediously and ignorantly." To Hugh Kenner, the women are "trivial." John Crowe Ransom, discerning "contempt" in Eliot's voice, rephrases the couplet as a rhetorical question about the women: "How could they have had any inkling of that glory which Michelangelo had put into his marbles and his paintings?"

Yet, as Ricks observes, nowhere does Eliot tell us how to react to these women entering and leaving the drawing room. He chooses "talking" to describe what they are doing when he could as easily have said "prattling." He uses no adjective to denigrate the women, though at his disposal he had those I've already given ("trivial," "ignorant," "tedious") and more ("shallow," "affected," "fashionable"). Nor does Eliot praise the "glory" of Michelangelo's "giant art" by way of emphasizing the discrepancy between the women and the object of their conversation. It is a measure of Eliot's subtlety and skill that he disdains such modifiers as would bully a reader into the desired response. But Ricks's larger point is that even redoubtable critics are unaware of "how much their sense of the lines is incited by prejudice."

Ricks's treatment of Eliot illustrates how canny a close reader he is. It may remind us also of the pleasure to be had from such acts of critical acumen. And if, as Wordsworth insisted in the preface to the *Lyrical Ballads,* the giving of pleasure constitutes the poet's first obligation to the reader, may it not be reasonable to expect the critic of poetry to honor this same imperative? Yet what Wordsworth calls the "grand elementary principle of pleasure" is missing from discussions of contemporary poetry. Schadenfreude is a poor substitute. True delight accompanies edification when a lover of poetry shows us how to read a poem on its own terms, paying it the respect of careful attention, leaving aside the prejudices of the anathematist, the ideologue, the apostle of received opinion, or the bully on the block.

It may just be that the most appealing alternative to the negativity of contemporary criticism is the selective inclusiveness of a dedicated editor. For thirty-six years David Wagoner edited *Poetry Northwest.* The value of a supportive editor is incalculable, and Wagoner was among the best. His editorial practice can be seen as an extension of his humane poetics. For more than a half century, he has written about ordinary lives and real landscapes with grace and emotional complexity. A master of the plain style, for whom clarity and directness are cardinal virtues, he is a poet of wisdom and wonder. In their unostentatious way, his poems remind us of what it means to be human. Although we set our sights on the heavens, what we see from the wrong end of the telescope may prove more vital, for it "shows us just how little the gods see / if they look back." Yet like actors in a grand comedy we turn and change, turn and change, "like young heavenly objects / endlessly reembodied" with "wardrobes as various / as the wonders of new stars." I am conflating quotations from two poems in Wagoner's latest collection,

A Map of the Night, which appeared last year—the year Wagoner spent reading for *The Best American Poetry 2009.* He has selected poems from an unprecedented number of print or electronic journals: fifty-six. The poets explore subjects ranging from love and death to God, Freud, the beauty of the matriarchs in Genesis, the animals with which we share the planet, "the land to the south of our neighbors to the north," the movies, and "The Great American Poem." A number of the poets address crises in the body politic: the damaged Mississippi Gulf Coast ("Liturgy"), the assassination of Daniel Pearl ("Forty"), the massacre at Virginia Tech ("Ringtone"). We read about the prospect of a change in government ("A Sea-Change") and are confronted with "A Democratic Vista" and the assurance that "Ultimately Justice Directs Them."

The biggest political story of 2008, the campaign and election of Barack Obama as president of the United States, sparked great enthusiasm among American poets. No sooner had the election results come in than the speculation began as to whom the incoming administration would tap to read a poem at the inauguration. Only two previous presidents (Kennedy and Clinton) had incorporated a poem in the inaugural proceedings, but everyone was confident that Obama would renew this tradition and everyone was right. Elizabeth Alexander was entrusted with the task. But even after her name was disclosed, the print and broadcast media continued to run stories on the importance of poetry in the national discourse. Perusal of the poems written by U.S. presidents of the past revealed Lincoln to be our best presidential poet. Anecdotes surfaced on Theodore Roosevelt's admiration of Edwin Arlington Robinson and Franklin Delano Roosevelt's recognition of Archibald MacLeish's talents as a speechwriter, librarian, and adviser at large. The Associated Press reporter Nancy Benac asked a number of poets to write—and, where practicable, recite for the camera—ceremonial poems written with Obama's inauguration in mind. Billy Collins, Yusef Komunyakaa, Alice Walker, Christopher Funkhouser, Amiri Baraka, cowboy poet Ted Newman, Julia Alvarez, Gary Soto, Bob Holman, and I composed poems for the occasion. The results are still accessible via the Internet.

The Internet has multiplied the number of places in which a poem may appear. If it was difficult previously to cover American poetry, even with a company of skillful readers, it is now quite impossible. As David Wagoner notes in his introduction to this year's *Best American Poetry,* there are more venues for poetry than ever before. Web sites, zines, and blogs have enabled us to close up the lag between the composition and dissemination of any piece of writing. It remains to be seen how this technological advance will affect the nature of the writing itself, although the odds are that it will abet not only the tendency toward informality but also the impulse to buck it by emphasizing new and unusual forms: the abecedarius (or double abecedarius), the lipogram, the use of "found forms" such as the index of first lines in the back of a book of poems. Poems in such forms as these have turned up in recent and current volumes of *The Best American Poetry,* as have, to be sure, sonnets, sestinas, riddles, prose poems, a villanelle, a cento, a blues poem, a pantoum. The rediscovery of old forms and the fabrication of new ones is one notable tendency in contemporary poetry. A second is the growing appeal of the conversational style that David Kirby calls "ultra talk": a poem that sounds as natural as talk—if we could script our talk. After observing that "every revolution in poetry" is at base "a return to common speech," T. S. Eliot in "The Music of Poetry" (1942) goes on to give the rationale for this sort of "talk poetry": "No poetry, of course, is ever exactly the same speech that the poet talks and hears: but it has to be in such a relation to the speech of his time that the listener or reader can say 'that is how I should talk if I could talk poetry.'"

In 2008, *The Best American Poetry* launched our blog, which seemed at first to be an indulgence, then a convenience, before we understood that it could function as a kind of magazine, the contents of which change daily and feature an ever-changing roster of contributing writers and columnists. We post poems and comments on poems but also news, links, photos, illustrations, and prose on any subject that engages the mind of a poet. There are certain recurring features. We like aphorisms ("There are people who are too intelligent to become authors, but they do not become critics": W. H. Auden) and brainteasers ("Lives in winter, / Dies in summer, / And grows with its root upwards").[4] From time to time we have run contests. Mark Strand judged Gerald Greland the winner of the inaugural ode contest we posted a day or two after Barack Obama's electoral victory. Paul Violi judged Frank Osen the winner of the previous year's competition, in which contestants were asked to decipher an anagram and to write an acrostic poem based on

---

4. "When a riddler, using the bold weapon of metaphor, forces us to contemplate an icicle *as* a plant, it is an imaginative coup; briefly, and in a small way, our sense of the structure of reality is shaken." Richard Wilbur, "The Persistence of Riddles" in *The Catbird's Song: Prose Pieces 1963–1995* (New York: Harcourt Brace, 1997), p. 44.

the result. I am still marveling at the notion that, in contrast to the strict limitations of space in a print magazine, we can publish 365 poems in a calendar year. And we can do things like monitor the cultural markers on an acclaimed television show.

The spirit of Frank O'Hara hovered over the second season of the TV series *Mad Men* on AMC in 2008. In the first episode, ad man Don Draper (played by Jon Hamm) finds himself at a Midtown bar not far from where O'Hara loitered during his lunch hours when he worked as a curator at the Museum of Modern Art. On the barstool next to Draper sits a man with horn-rimmed glasses and curly hair reading O'Hara's *Meditations in an Emergency*. It is 1962. John F. Kennedy is president. Marilyn Monroe is still alive. Draper asks the man about the book. "You probably wouldn't like it," he is told. But Don buys it, we see him reading it in his office, and as the episode concludes, he mails the book to person or persons unknown and, in a voice-over, recites the fourth and final part of O'Hara's poem "Mayakovsky" in *Meditations in an Emergency*. The unforgettable phrase "the catastrophe of my personality" occurs here. The charm of such ironic self-deprecation, which is part of O'Hara's character armor, extends to the voice-over. The last words in "Mayakovsky" imply a split in the speaker's personality: "It may be the coldest day of / the year, what does he think of / that? I mean, what do I? And if I do, / perhaps I am myself again." The grammatical fact that, in a narrative, the same person can be either "I" or "he" turns into an apt metaphor for Don Draper, who bears someone else's name—he switched identities (we learned in season one) with a fallen comrade in a skirmish during the Korean War.

Meditations in an Emergency returns as the title of the thirteenth and final episode in season two of *Mad Men*. Marilyn Monroe has died. It is October. President Kennedy is addressing the nation on TV. Virtually all the characters in the show are going through an emergency of one kind or another, while the country as a whole faces the grave emergency that was the Cuban Missile Crisis. Unlike radio, which has always been a congenial medium for poems and verse plays, TV and poetry have seemed as irreconcilable as dance and architecture. Not the least of Matthew Weiner's accomplishments is the brilliant way he has used O'Hara's poetry to govern the themes of a dramatic series on TV. *Mad Men* is a big hit, sales of *Meditations in an Emergency* continue to climb, and a new generation of readers has fallen in love with the poems of Frank O'Hara.

David Wagoner was born in Massillon, Ohio, in 1926, the son of a steel-mill worker. He grew up in Ohio and Indiana. As an undergraduate at Penn State he studied with Theodore Roethke. After working briefly as a reporter, he joined Roethke on the faculty of the University of Washington in 1954. His most recent book of poems is *A Map of the Night* (University of Illinois Press, 2008). He is the author of eighteen other collections, including *The House of Song, Good Morning and Good Night,* and *Traveling Light: Collected and New Poems* (University of Illinois Press, 1999). He has also written ten novels, including *The Escape Artist* (1965), which Francis Ford Coppola adapted into a movie. He edited *Straw for the Fire: From the Notebooks of Theodore Roethke, 1943–63* (1972) and wrote a one-person play about Roethke, *First Class,* that had a six-week run in Seattle in the summer of 2007. A former Chancellor of the Academy of American Poets, Wagoner was the editor in chief of *Poetry Northwest* from 1966 until its last issue in 2002. He has received an American Academy of Arts and Letters award, the Ruth Lilly Poetry Prize, and fellowships from the Ford Foundation, the Guggenheim Foundation, and the National Endowment for the Arts. He is an emeritus professor at the University of Washington in Seattle and lives in Lynnwood, Washington.

INTRODUCTION

by David Wagoner

◊　◊　◊

A few months ago I was interviewed by a Seattle TV station for reasons having nothing to do with poetry, and the interviewer made a side excursion and asked whether it wasn't sort of depressing to be as involved as I am with American poetry when it was generally ignored by the literate public. She asked offhandedly as if the answer were so obvious, she hardly needed to wait for it.

She seemed genuinely surprised and slightly offended when I laughed and disagreed and changed the subject as soon as it was polite to do so. At the time, I was knee-deep in literary magazines, trying to keep up with the most recent work of American poets, hunting for the seventy-five poems you're holding in your hands. I don't know how widespread her impression is. There are, no doubt, a multitude of poets who feel at least slightly neglected, but I'm sure most of them realize that readers of all kinds are paying a great deal of desirable attention to many other poets, perhaps more so than ever before in the annals of American literature.

When I began submitting poems to magazines as a graduate student—World War II had ended two years earlier—I had only a few places to aim for: *Poetry, Harper's, The Atlantic Monthly, The Yale Review, Partisan Review, Sewanee Review, The Saturday Review,* the *Virginia Quarterly Review, Accent* (I'm straining to remember now, and I'm sure others will remember for me); perhaps *The Iowa Review* had begun, and *Prairie Schooner,* but almost nothing else west of the Mississippi, though there was a cluster of very small journals published by college English departments here and there around the country. No doubt there were fewer poets competing then, but the outlets for new work were minute compared with today's opportunities for publication. I won't go into the jungle of self-publishing. And I'm not even going to try to guess how many magazines there are now, not even counting online venues. By the time I reached the deadline of November 30, 2008, I felt certain that if a poet of even the most modest talent couldn't get published (free of charge) today, he or she just wasn't trying.

At the end of World War II, it seemed to dawn simultaneously on the heads of English departments in colleges and universities from coast to coast that they weren't teaching creative writing or, if they happened to have a course or two like that, they weren't offering a degree in it and perhaps they ought to think about it. Several Ivy League schools had been doing it for a while: the University of Michigan, the University of North Carolina, the University of Iowa, and a few other daring departments here and there had taken a chance, and fortunately for me, Indiana University joined the small bunch in 1948, brought in Peter Taylor to run it, brought in Stephen Spender, Karl Shapiro, and John Frederick Nims to conduct a Young Writers' Conference to inaugurate it, and I was its first graduate soon after.

The GI Bill changed the whole atmosphere of American education, and throughout the 1950s, the practice of inviting poets into classrooms changed the character of high school English classes for the better. Students learned early to recognize what was corny and to realize that the language they were using every day was the stuff of poetry, too. To use myself as an example of how poorly standard textbooks prepared one for literature: as a senior English major at Penn State in 1947, I stepped into Theodore Roethke's poetry workshop having read exactly two poems by living poets. They were Carl Sandburg's "Jazz Fantasia," which I thought was so bad, I refused to read it aloud to the class when my high school teacher told me to do so, and Eliot's "The Hollow Men," which I had run across accidentally in a book (not a textbook) belonging to the parents of a friend.

I don't know how to explain the sudden burgeoning of American women poets during that time, but from the mid-fifties on, the statistics show a more and more nearly equal representation of women in magazines and anthologies, and their value and influence today is no longer secondary or exceptional.

On December 1, 2007, the first day this anthology was assigned to cover, I submitted poems of mine to fifty American magazines. I hadn't been sending out work recently and had been prolific for a while, and I thought I'd find out how prompt the poetry editors in this country were being nowadays. The prizewinner—John Tait of the Texas-based *American Literary Review*—took only four days to reply. After three months, I'd heard from one-third. After six months, I'd heard from a little over half. The losers are the nine magazines who still haven't replied, though thirteen months have passed. The editors in this last group are difficult to excuse. Whatever may be interfering with their decision making is making creative life tough for poets, especially for the young who need critical judgment of their work, both for encouragement and for help in improving it, and the sooner, the better. It's no wonder many poets have turned to multiple submissions: sending the same set of poems to two or more magazines at the same time.

I edited *Poetry Northwest* for thirty-six years and made it my policy early on not to consider multiples if I could help it. I also made it my policy not to make any poet wait longer than a month—usually it was closer to two weeks—for a decision. But I became more and more lenient as the years went by and I learned how long most other editors were making poets wait. Why can't editors make up their minds sooner? This is the commonest theme in letters and e-mails I receive from former students and from *Poetry Northwest* contributors. Undoubtedly there are many excuses for the long months these aspiring poets spend in the equivalent of waiting rooms, vestibules, on airport benches, in ticket lines, and holding cells. The struggle between poets and editors has reached a kind of stalemate now, and I've heard strong opinions on both sides. It seems clear, to me at least, that it's the editors alone who can improve the situation, and also that it's their responsibility to do so.

During my time as editor, I watched rhyme virtually disappear from the submitted poems. Fewer than one in a hundred used that once nearly required device any longer, and free verse outnumbered metrical poems more and more overwhelmingly. The poems I read in order to make this anthology explored nearly every nook and cranny between formal versification and prose and broke every so-called rule in the history of prosody. I'm sure if some new ringmaster, some new manifestation of a literary dictator, would appear on the scene, many of today's poets would be extremely grateful to him or her and would set about breaking any of the new strictures and decrees as soon and as thoroughly as possible. After World War I and till the end of World War II, if a poet wasn't in an anthology put together by Louis Untermeyer or Oscar Williams, he or she wasn't in the running. There is no such overseer of reputations today, though David Lehman may come as close to qualifying as anyone else I can think of. I've had a small share of that diminished authority during the past year, and I'm both grateful for it and a little afraid of it and I am glad it's over. The Internet and the ease of self-publishing and self-promotion and the proliferation of less comprehensive anthologies have made the old ways nearly impossible.

Why do people write poems? There are probably a hundred answers to that question, maybe more, but some writers feel they have important messages to give mankind, and of course they usually turn out to be strangely inaudible to that vast audience. Some people just like to play around with words as they might with jigsaw puzzles or pinball machines. Some indulge themselves with poetry secretly, in words as private as diary entries. For some it's a form of public speaking, and they look for audiences in social clubs, or open mikes, or even on street corners, making themselves heard to strangers. Some hear their own voices and the voices of other people speaking to them in half sleep and feel obliged to write down what they say in order to understand their own existence more fully. For a number of them what starts out to be a kind of game turns out to be the most complex and rewarding of all game-like activities, something more nearly religious, as demanding and baffling and compelling as ethics, metaphysics, the search for a god, or even love.

I found many poems in print—both in established journals and in more hairy, "experimental," often one-shot publications—that Auden would have called "imaginary poems," a term he applied to verse in which the poet had left most of the creative work to the reader and had failed to supply enough building materials to allow even that much to happen. But the majority of the poems that caught my eye were genuine efforts to fulfill the traditional duties of the poet as maker and master craftsman.

Though I tried hard, I'm sure I didn't even come close to reading all the poems published in magazines this past year. I received subscriptions to many of them, and a number of friends sent me what they'd admired, and David Lehman and several of his scouts sent me tear sheets and Xeroxes of what had impressed them. But in the long run, I'm responsible for all the choices.

To those who feel unfairly left out, I must say I could easily have chosen seventy-five other poems and been nearly as proud of that selection as I am of this. Many, many really good poems are coming out of every area of the country, and there's no reason to suppose it will be any different next year, the year after, and for decades to come.

Many English and American poets of the past, some of whom wrote and published hundreds of poems in their lifetimes and were admired and praised for them, are now routinely remembered by and reduced to one or two poems by textbook editors and anthologists, and the rest of their work is left to specialists and scholars. Randall Jarrell said, "A poet is a man"—he would be stoned for that today—"who manages, in a lifetime of standing out in a thunderstorm, to be struck by lightning five or six times." He was being a little more generous in numbers than I. Many poets today are aware that their lifetime labors may result in just such a reduction, and they may never know which one or two of their works may put a laurel crown on their heads after they've gone. The seventy-five in this anthology, for all we or they know, may include one or more of those bits of immortality. They've made the first step anyway by being singled out from among thousands.

Why do we feel some poems are better than others? It seems like a simple question, but it goes to the heart of many matters, including: What is a poem? Dylan Thomas dodged the question when he said that poems are statements made on the way to the grave. A. E. Houseman said that poetry was what made him cut himself if he thought of the lines while shaving. Wordsworth's "spontaneous overflow of powerful feelings," his "emotion recollected in tranquility," have taken up a lot of space in the search for an agreeable definition, though most poets have doubted the tranquility. Some have settled for the blunt, simple definition: Memorable speech. Others have called poems a by-product of the game of knowledge. Dictionaries fumble around with the words "composition," "beauty," and "imagination," and once in a while, tentatively, murmur the word "rhythm," but get away from it as soon as possible.

Auden was terse: "One demands two things of a poem. Firstly, it must be a well-made verbal object that does honor to the language in which it is written. Secondly, it must say something significant about a reality common to us all, but perceived from a unique perspective. What the poet says has never been said before, but, once he has said it, his readers recognize its validity for themselves." When I read this aloud, I have the same feeling I often have in the classroom. When I hear myself uttering some flat-out pronouncement about the nature and effects of poetry, a voice behind my semicircular canals mutters, "Yes, but the opposite is also true." Must a good poem be well made? The definition of that term has varied wildly over the years. What is significant to one generation may be insignificant to the next. Are there no uncommon realities yet to be written about? If a good poem must come from a unique perspective, what about those poems by Auden like "September 1, 1939" that gave him the label of "spokesman for a whole generation"? Must a good poem say what has never been said before? Not according to many respected critics nor to many good poets themselves. And as for Wordsworth's "spontaneous overflow of powerful feelings," his "emotion recollected in tranquility," isn't it just as likely that poems can come from deliberately induced, dried-out absorptions of barely discernible impressions mostly half forgotten in ecstasy?

Many definitions of poetry mention lyricism and beautiful or meaningful sounds but don't go into the subject very deeply because such matters are difficult to describe, especially by teachers with insensitive ears. My high school speech teacher—there used to be such beings in northern Indiana—used to warm up our enunciation by having us recite: "He thrusts his fists against the posts / And still insists he sees the ghosts," which I suppose is also an example of bad poetry. In *Tom Thumb,* Henry Fielding satirizes bad, earless playwrights by having Princess Huncmunca say "The pretty little fleecy bleating sheep," among other screechy lines. Sandburg's frequently quoted "Poetry is the essence of hyacinths and biscuits" is an inadvertent tongue twister that Fielding would have admired. I wager there would be more general agreement among readers about which poems are really bad than about which are really good.

I heard John Ciardi say that, as the longtime poetry editor of *Saturday Review,* he didn't have to read beyond the first line of any submission to know whether it would be possible to publish what he was looking at. I consider that an extreme position and would, from long experience, say three lines. But editors are probably much more impatient than general readers of poetry, who don't have to judge a poem if they don't feel like it. Editors and teachers of workshops and, of course, the poets themselves in revision have to think about aspects of the craft in detail, usually right down to individual syllables, while general readers enjoy (or fail to enjoy) the effects of a poem in a more open way. If asked, they are likely to praise or find fault with imagery, dramatic order, originality, surprise, deep emotion, shocks of recognition, and so on. But even many general readers may emulate John Ciardi halfway through a poem and discard it if the poet isn't keeping his or her promises.

A student in a poetry workshop came up to me before class one day and said, "I wrote a poem two days ago and thought it was great. I read it this morning, and it seems like nothing. How can I tell if I'm right or wrong?" It's an old question, and it's always been hard to answer. Almost all poets have had trouble judging their own work, except those few—Robert Frost reputedly among them—who have felt their every line was worthy of being inscribed in beaten gold on the Everlasting Gates. Most learn not to judge their own work, or anyone else's, when they're tired or exasperated or otherwise not in a judicious frame of mind. In choosing the poems for this anthology, I tried, as much as time allowed, to let my opinions age, to consider more than twice which poems showed the greatest mastery of the skills in workmanship, the most inventiveness, the greatest fulfillment of a reader's expectations.

Poetry began out of necessity, out of irresistible impulse among preliterate peoples. It began together with song and dance around the campfire, out of grief at the sides of graves, out of the boasting and fear and hunger and the search for power before and after the hunt and making war and love. If it were all to disappear from books and magazines now, out of our libraries, out of our memories, the poets among us would begin all over again inventing it, shaping it, speaking it, writing it down, and I'm certain, after a half-dozen generations, poems would be enriching American speech and our lives once more.

While advertisers and local, national, and international manipulators of "truth" and outright liars are doing their Orwellian best to make language do their bidding and earn them money or power, poets and other writers are doing their damnedest to keep the language strong and vital in the exploration, the growth, and the sustenance of the human spirit, to help keep it from becoming a self-destructive monstrosity.

THE
BEST
AMERICAN
POETRY
2009

◇ ◇ ◇

JOHN ASHBERY

They Knew What They Wanted

◇   ◇   ◇

They all kissed the bride.
They all laughed.
They came from beyond space.
They came by night.

They came to a city.
They came to blow up America.
They came to rob Las Vegas.
They dare not love.

They died with their boots on.
They shoot horses, don't they?
They go boom.
They got me covered.

They flew alone.
They gave him a gun.
They just had to get married.
They live. They loved life.

They live by night.
They drive by night.
They knew Mr. Knight.
They were expendable.

They met in Argentina.
They met in Bombay.
They met in the dark.
They might be giants.

They made me a fugitive.
They made me a criminal.
They only kill their masters.
They shall have music.

They were sisters.
They still call me Bruce.
They won't believe me.
They won't forget.

from *London Review of Books* and *Vanitas*

Beasts and Violins

◇   ◇   ◇

I wandered the house looking for a blank notebook
today, until I found one of the small spiral ones
I prefer. It had tacky shots of mountain climbers
on the cover, and read "Dig In!" with bright letters.
I don't prefer the styling, but appreciate the portability.
And though it was in my house, the notebook
wasn't mine, and wasn't empty.

Inside it had lists. Lists of bands, places, problems
—with notes detailing why my ex-girlfriend was unhappy.
My name appeared on most pages. It was hers,
left on a bookshelf for over one year.
She always kept lists, as if her life could be categorized
into columns of good and bad, written repeatedly
like an incantation, banishment spell, or scale.

There was a section detailing which albums
were best of the year, another with her all-time favorite
movies. One more with the pros and cons
of her parents, and a paragraph on how
I was controlling and didn't care. There was a travelogue
of notable locations in the desert Southwest,
filled out with names of people we had known
in a little town. I even found some suggestions
that, by now, she was only with me for the dogs.

Still, it was only a quarter full of this shit,
and I wanted the notebook. So I ripped out her pages,
stuck them in the winter fire. It made me

happy. Filled me up, like I was drunk
in a train-car lounge, and every time I checked my wallet,
I would find another twenty. Maybe there
would be weeper country music playing
and I'd be hoping the fiddle would take the melody,
and in the last thirty seconds, it would.
The suspense would all be worth it. The heartache
would become transcendent. I'd jump
off my stool and dance right there on the train.
The snow would be too high for the wolves
to give chase. Their eyes would cut tree limbs
as they raised their heads to howl.

from *Poet Lore*

Concerning the Land to the South of Our Neighbors to the North

◊   ◊   ◊

How does it feel, Hawaii, to be first, for a change?

The state bird of Delaware flies too fast to be identified—
see, it's already over Nebraska, booming a sonic boom.

Comprised of two ovals, Michigan is known as The Infinity State.

Illinois has some imposing adult stores along the railway.

West Virginia was made overseas and brought to us, chunk by chunk,
        aboard container ships.

During his final days, Hiram Warren Johnson, governor of California
        from 1911 to 1917, subsisted on scorpions and grapes.

No one could have foreseen what a handful Utah would become, influenced
as it is by the contrarian zephyrs of New Hampshire, three states away.

Scientists predict that Colorado will soon be an archipelago,
though not in our lifetime, and Florida shall turn dusty
as the Necco Wafers scattered nightly across Massachusetts.

It is the custom in Maryland to honor the stegosaurus on Stegosaurus Day.

Not even the kimchi of Oregon can rival
the kimchi produced in South Dakota.

Knock knock who's there Texas Texas who no just Texas.

Before it was written, my novel was banned in Rhode Island on account of
the unions.

New Jersey, did you know that one of your shoulders was queer?

The night sky over Iowa resembles flannel, the moon a fluctuating stain.

Engorged fleas of Missouri bounce across the land, crushing all in their path.

Has anyone seen Tennessee? It was here a minute ago.

Nevada has kind of a shitty homepage, but not
as bad as that of Arkansas, which lists "Deposit to Inmate Bank Accounts" as
one of its top five online services.

Washington is rich in natural anagrams.

In the deep and frigid caves of Arizona live fish that started
out in Kansas and got lost on their way to the sea.

Wearing boxer briefs in Oklahoma will net you a $40 fine, while
the penalty for mixed metaphors in Vermont is garroting;
of course, if you're heard saying "You go, girl" in Alaska, that's two months'
community service.

Minnesota, can we borrow some brown sugar?

Indiana has a tail—Jesus, a tail!

As in Andorra, the main environmental hazard of Pennsylvania is avalanches,
while overgrazing has decimated nearly half of Maine.

New York remains, alas, the only state without a capital.

SOUTH CAROLINA SURE LOOKS DELICIOUS appears on every license plate
in North Carolina.

Wisconsin blames its financial woes on shady investment deals involving a
	chain of make-your-own-scrapple emporia.

Trust me, you do not want to get arrested in Georgia.

Nothing else sticks in your teeth like Wyoming's nostalgia.

The limbo, thought by many to have been invented in Louisiana,
can in fact trace its roots to New Mexico.

Existential and Persnickety are small towns in Ohio, and would you
believe the state fish of Montana is the blackspotted cutthroat trout?

. . . Idaho . . .

Mississippi means *gesundheit* in Esperanto.

Satellite images of North Dakota look pretty much like you'd expect, and one
can only avoid Virginia for so long.

Speaking of arcane delicacies, Pewee Valley, Kentucky (pop. 1,436), is famous
	for a dish called leather pie.

Well, this is the first I've heard of Alabama.

Connecticut! we're sawing you in half.

from *La Petite Zine*

Ringtone

◊　◊　◊

As they loaded the dead onto the gurneys
to wheel them from the university halls,
who could have predicted the startled chirping
in those pockets, the invisible bells
and tiny metal music of the phones,
in each the cheer of a voiceless song.
Pop mostly, Timberlake, Shakira, tunes
never more various now, more young,
shibboleths of what a student hears,
what chimes in the doorway to the parent
on the line. Who could have answered there
in proxy for the dead, received the panic
with grace, however artless, a live bird
gone still at the meeting of the strangers.

from *Ploughshares*

The Doctor

◇　◇　◇

I read bodies, she says. So I
show her what I was
given, trusted with, wake
up to, tell her where
and what, which arm or leg, which
ache near dawn,
the flash at the back of the skull,
a narrowing in muscle
or bone or nerve
that makes it a city suddenly
built so badly, so far
from the sea, first a rumor
then after, such photos
to carry about, tiresome
drone of travel there repeated
endlessly, variation
chilling to theme, news
that comes back as I try
to remember, to tell her
whatever. And she reads
with stethoscope and glove, a tiny
light for those dizzying
channels in the head, looking up
or into, locking my joints then
unlocking them slowly
or quick: look left—good—look
right, lie down, breathe
shallow, now deep. To say
Braille would be putting it all

into dark. But what goes on
is mindless, brilliant
pulse where wrist
is most bluish, the skin a veil,
bones the thinnest shuttle
crossing, recrossing.
Her questions: how long? or
when-I-press-this and do you feel it
dull or sharp? And can she
believe me or this country
she's never seen, never been to?
Maybe it's familiar, this place.
She might know
the language, she might,
of its slow, well-meaning
citizens, most of whom don't want
to come out of their houses, ever.
Really, a simple quiet room
would do. And please,
a small-to-medium bowl
of something.

from *The Cincinnati Review*

Roofers

◇   ◇   ◇

Five roofers are wedging off the old,
scraping it over the edge. Great black birds
diving in front of the window.
In another place, a nail gun goes off in patterns
of four, sometimes five. They're nice guys:
one has a funny beard that sticks
straight out, one has a lip ring. One is pounding,
testing for rot. One is flipping the sections of shingles
down: I hear them slap like clown's feet,
something out of Shakespeare. These guys know
what they're doing and they do it,
great rolls of thunder, the roof
of heaven cluttered with gods: Homer's
Tityus, Leto, Tantalus—the ones
who work the obscure jobs, who come
when called, the ones before Milton's great-
voiced dignitary, before Hopkins's rod bearer,
the ones from the old days, from my old days,
when over my head there was music
in the air, the pitch of my church-camp voice
raised out of the heat and the breeze
and the sun on the spillway rocks, all of it
holding me in as if I were in a shadow box,
the kind where someone looks through
a peephole and everything is 3-D, so the eye
is like the Important God. I am filled

with tenderness for the little world I had going on inside, my grief that it was not the world.

from *The Georgia Review*

The Book of Steve

◊   ◊   ◊

"God made Adam and Eve, not Adam and Steve."

But what if God did? What if I showed you
the lost book in that cramped hand some call Moses',
right to left (you read Hebrew, right?), the Book of Steve?
Stefan, if you're Orthodox, Esteban
if you also worship the Virgin of Guadalupe,
but never mind those dark madonnas. The Book of Steve:
it's much like the rest of the Pentateuch, you'll recognize
the style, except that it was before Genesis 1
when Steve became a living soul. A lively, friendly soul:
when those animals came questing, Steve was thrilled.
He scratched their ears as he named them, pulled
their ticks, asked them what they thought they should be called.
So he was scratching and chatting, naming away,
when up came Adam (Yahweh had been practicing men).
"Hey, dude." "Hey, Adam. You think this looks
like a crocodile?" "I dunno. More like a fox?"
They had a few beers (Yahweh's work of the day),
named five kinds of ants: Steve got carpenter,
leaf-cutter, sugar; Adam took fire and soldier.
Probably they made love, probably a lot (the world
was young then), but the Book of Steve is demure;
Moses, or someone, drew the curtain of discretion.

When the curtain comes up, the snake
still has brief feet, but Adam is changing the names
to better ones, and Steve's not there. It seems
there were complaints. Steve talked too much, always on

about feelings, food, the slant of the light; sometimes
he wanted to be on top; he took the remote, and didn't
give it back when Adam glared. And his chest wasn't nearly
enough like a pillow. It was all too much.

The end of the book is torn out; there are marks of fire.
No one knows who defiled the Book of Steve,
but in some stories it is said that Eden has other quadrants
and that Steve is in one of them.
Steve, and the snakes with feet, and other people
who missed the next book: the roc preening its iridescent plumes,
the unicorn lipping apples, the manticore having a dustbath.
They say that somewhere among the leaves of western Eden
was found a helpmeet for Steve, who was not fruitful,
who did not multiply, who had no dominion over the earth.

from *Asheville Poetry Review*

SUZANNE CLEARY

From The Boy's Own Book: A Compleat Encyclopedia of All the Diversions Athletic, Scientific, and Recreative, of Boyhood and Youth, *by William Clarke*

◊   ◊   ◊

William Clarke would have us believe
time rests lightly on the boy of 1829,
light as a penny placed atop the hand,

the hand pulled suddenly out, and turned
so as to catch the penny
before it hits the ground,

a trick with nearly endless
variations: penny placed on the forehead,
the elbow, the knee, *etcetera*.

Gravity is a game to the boy of 1829,
even as he learns to chop wood,
to shoot birds out of the sky.

The weight of his own body
may provide him hours of delight,
as in jumping over a trench,

vaulting over a wooden horse,
or performing what William Clarke names
The Deep Leap, wherein the boy stands

on a flight of stairs, jumps
clear to the floor. Clarke adds, *We do not, however,
much approve of this exercise,*

in his 300-page compendium this comment
a rare appearance of Clarke's own voice,
such that from this point forward

one boy understands Clarke's silence as tacit approval
of the tricks involving fire or knives or even glass,
which is dear and likely to shatter

if instructions are not followed
precisely, this boy most likely a bookworm
interested in *Card Tricks, Arithmetical Dazzlers,*

the thick chapter *Riddles and Puns,*
wherein words shift shape
like smoke relighting the candle.

This is the boy who will grow
to be the tallest man in the county
while his daredevil brother, come spring,
will take the fever, and die.

Why is a pack of cards like a garden?
Why is sealing wax like a soldier?
Why is a man like a burning candle?

What is the weight of the moon?

from *Margie: The American Journal of Poetry*

The Great American Poem

◇   ◇   ◇

If this were a novel,
it would begin with a character,
a man alone on a southbound train
or a young girl on a swing by a farmhouse.

And as the pages turned, you would be told
that it was morning or the dead of night,
and I, the narrator, would describe
for you the miscellaneous clouds over the farmhouse

and what the man was wearing on the train
right down to his red tartan scarf,
and the hat he tossed onto the rack above his head,
as well as the cows sliding past his window.

Eventually—one can only read so fast—
you would learn either that the train was bearing
the man back to the place of his birth
or that he was headed into the vast unknown,

and you might just tolerate all of this
as you waited patiently for shots to ring out
in a ravine where the man was hiding
or for a tall, raven-haired woman to appear in a doorway.

But this is a poem, not a novel,
and the only characters here are you and I,
alone in an imaginary room
which will disappear after a few more lines,

leaving us no time to point guns at one another
or toss all our clothes into a roaring fireplace.
I ask you: who needs the man on the train
and who cares what his black valise contains?

We have something better than all this turbulence
lurching toward some ruinous conclusion.
I mean the sound that we will hear
as soon as I stop writing and put down this pen.

I once heard someone compare it
to the sound of crickets in a field of wheat
or, more faintly, just the wind
over that field stirring things that we will never see.

from *The Virginia Quarterly Review*

ROB COOK

The Song of America

◊ ◊ ◊

I'm raising my child to become the end of rotting,
      and to expose the lushness of the cemetery moth.
I'm raising my child to know the difference between the two sunsets:
      one purple with thermonuclear iodine,
      the other the charred insides of rain.
I'm raising my child to find the stones his brothers fed each other.
I'm raising my child to fall behind the apricot blossoms
      and to trust only others who've fallen behind.
I'm raising my child to listen: there is so much noise
      only silence will be remembered.
I'm raising my child to fill in the spaces between wars
      and the spaces between people
      where everything grows even after the last space is gone.
I'm raising my child to bring into the world books that suffer
      with words detention-kids make over and over.
I'm raising my child to follow the scatter of flesh across the sky,
      birds and their wingprint trails to Alaska.
I'm raising my child to predict the sicknesses left of summer
      by the number of shadows he sweats.
I'm raising my child to plant pennies where he'll find rest
      and good fingerpaint for one night.
I'm raising my child to chop down the televisions of peasants
      and their machine that picks thunderstorms from a leaf.
I'm raising my child to write a treaty for his own smells,
      the ones that hurt the self and the ones that hurt others,
      and a treaty for the poison sumac whose only emotion is hunger.
I'm raising my child to dress like a long line of near-humans
      if he wants to be recognized
      and to show kindness to the roadkill that sneaks into his bed.

I'm raising my child to know which part of a hamburger is still afraid.
I'm raising my child to be captain of the abandoned mail trucks
        and to lead the grasses across the Midwestern sleep.
I'm raising my child to leave New York.
I'm raising my child to add letters and numbers to his name
        and chameleons and hellbenders behind his name.
I'm raising my child to drown and to drop dead and to carry buildings on his back.
I'm raising my child to listen to his face breaking when it's cold.
I'm raising my child to seduce only photographs of women.
I'm raising my child to know that the cobras that shiver
        in the sky at night are mistakes and not responsible for us.
I'm raising my child to leave bread for the voices that come after dark.
I'm raising my child to keep his eyes closed.
I'm raising my child to tell the truth by having no sound at all.

                        from *Fence*

Freud

◇　◇　◇

Come to think of it, I never speak of Mom
much now, though I go on and on about Dad.
My generation's given "Mom" a beating,
I think: there's no son who hasn't got his gun
out for the old dear—the dear in the headlights!
Think it could be, like, you know, like . . . *Freud*?

Speaking of beatings, who's taken more than Freud,
lately? From the belly of "The Beast," not Mom's:
Shtand ze kike against zer vall! Aim ze headlights . . .
But why beat Freud instead of dear old Dad?
Dad's the one who's always pulling out his gun,
longing to give *someone* a "Christian" beating!

Freud got a few things wrong—that's worth a beating?
Let's whack some Christians instead of poor Freud.
It's clear they understand about "The Gun"—
but what about "The Cave"? No, no, not Mom's—
and let's not even go there about Dad's.
Their *zeitgeist* is a scramble toward headlights—

figures projected on a wall by headlights—
then, once there, instituting someone's beating.
How do you break it to your "real-life" Dad
that twenty centuries of this *schadenfreude*
are too much? That this smokescreen called "Mom"
just hides the cave of God-Our-Daddy's gun?

They co-opt Jesus into their hired gun—
that rabble-rousing Jewish kid, with head lice—
then claim he cut this strange deal with *his* Mom?
And he'll *return*—to give the "sons" a beating?
No wonder we're devouring poor old Freud!
We'll swallow any tale "revealed" by "Dad."

"I can sell you *anything*!" My own dad
points his shaking finger like a gun
at me. He wonders who the hell is Freud;
he winks and elbows me about "headlights."
His diaper leaks. His pride takes a beating.
I shoo him off to Florida with "Mom."

Amerika: a graveyard, a Mom-and-Dad
beating. Whistle past. Switch on your headlights.
A gun can *be* a gun, even for Freud.

from *The Antioch Review*

MARK DOTY

Apparition (Favorite Poem)

◇　◇　◇

The old words are dying,
everyone forgets them,
pages falling into sleep and dust,
dust and sleep, burning so slowly
you wouldn't even know there's a fire.
Or that's what I think half the time.
Then, at the bookstore, a young man reciting,
slight for fourteen, blond, without irony
but not self-important either;
his loping East Texas vowels threaten
to escape the fence of pentameter,
his voice seems to have just arrived here,
but the old cadence inhabits anyway.
He makes the poem his own
even as he becomes a vessel
for its reluctance to disappear.
All right, maybe they perish,
but the boy has the look of someone
repeating a crucial instruction
that must be delivered, word for word,
as he has learned it:
My name is Ozymandias, King of Kings,
Look on my Works, ye Mighty, and despair.

from *Five Points*

23

How It Will End

◇   ◇   ◇

We're walking on the boardwalk
but stop when we see a lifeguard and his girlfriend
fighting. We can't hear what they're saying,
but it is as good as a movie. We sit on a bench to find out
how it will end. I can tell by her body language
he's done something really bad. She stands at the bottom
of the ramp that leads to his hut. He tries to walk halfway down
to meet her, but she keeps signaling *Don't come closer.*
My husband says, "Boy, he's sure in for it,"
and I say, "He deserves whatever's coming to him."
My husband thinks the lifeguard's cheated, but I think
she's sick of him only working part-time
or maybe he forgot to put the rent in the mail.
The lifeguard tries to reach out
and she holds her hand like Diana Ross
when she performed "Stop in the Name of Love."
The red flag that slaps against his station means strong currents.
"She has to just get it out of her system,"
my husband laughs, but I'm not laughing.
I start to coach the girl to leave the no-good lifeguard,
but my husband predicts she'll never leave.
I'm angry at him for seeing glee in their situation
and say, "That's your problem—you think every fight
is funny. You never take her seriously," and he says,
"You never even give the guy a chance and you're always nagging,
so how can he tell the real issues from the nitpicking?"
and I say, "She doesn't nitpick!" and he says, "Oh really?
Maybe he should start recording her tirades," and I say
"Maybe he should help out more," and he says

"Maybe she should be more supportive," and I say
"Do you mean supportive or do you mean support him?"
and my husband says that he's doing the best he can,
that's he's a lifeguard for Christ's sake, and I say
that her job is much harder, that she's a waitress
who works nights carrying heavy trays and is hit on all the time
by creepy tourists and he just sits there most days napping
and listening to "Power 96" and then ooh
he gets to be the big hero blowing his whistle
and running into the water to save beach bunnies who flatter him
and my husband says it's not as though she's Miss Innocence
and what about the way she flirts, giving free refills
when her boss isn't looking or cutting extra large pieces of pie
to get bigger tips, oh no she wouldn't do that because she's a saint
and he's the devil, and I say, "I don't know why you can't just admit
he's a jerk," and my husband says, "I don't know why you can't admit
she's a killjoy," and then out of the blue the couple is making up.
The red flag flutters, then hangs limp.
She has her arms around his neck and is crying into his shoulder.
He whisks her up into his hut. We look around, but no one is watching us.

from *Barrow Street*

Getting Serious

◇   ◇   ◇

Today I started looking for my soul.
Yesterday it was my keys. Last week,
my brain which I couldn't find, it being out
looking for me, now that I'm getting so old.

First I thought my soul would have gone
back to Greece where she grew so tall and straight,
she thought she was a column. Or back to camp,
being forever twelve and underdeveloped.
Perhaps, being careless, I left her during the 70s
in bed with God knows whom. Or could be
I buried her with my mother—my head not being right—
but that was my heart.

So I went to where I know
I saw her last. Radio City Music Hall.
I'm six, my feet barely brushing the floor,
and the Rockettes start shuffling out, long-
legged and perfect as paper-dolls kicking up
down in a wave. One body with seventy-two knees
chugging like pistons going back in a forever mirror,
same as in Coney Island's Fun House or on Mama's can
of Dutch Cleanser. And my heart flexed in me, a sail,
and I swear I saw it flying out of my chest
spiriting away my giddy soul, ears plugged and tied
to the mast: *I can't hear you I can't hear you.*

from *Ploughshares*

MARGARET GIBSON

Black Snake

◊   ◊   ◊

1.

When, in the darkened room, I hear a clatter from the mantel
of the central chimney with its many chinks,
and turn to see why a plate has leapt to the floor on its own,
I freeze
          as a sleek thick ribbon of snake
slides like rain
over the rough stones of the chimney and into an opening
I swear is no wider
than the eye of my wedding ring.

And I understand Persephone at a standstill, just before
she swallows the single seed
on her complicit tongue—
                         and Orpheus, as he
turns and stares into the retreating pour of dark mist.

I have seen a black snake loop from an oak limb,
as cursive in the air
as a Chinese acrobat.

I've watched one meditate in the shade of the blue mist bush,
the thick lump in its long throat
slowly shrinking.

And in a corner of the summer attic, I've held in my hands
a snakeskin, torn at both ends,
rumpled at the head where it split and the snake

tugged free.
What is a snake,
that it casts off such transparent trappings? What is

this skin, in which
I find a nature that's empty, not unlike my own?

2.

Were I a loose swirl—a black water ripple—one continuous, long
throat,
what would be
the song I'd inscribe on stone, on ground, on grass?

No beginning to it, no end, snake comes through winter,
its tail in its mouth—
and a coil of song
issues from the deepest trance of its body.

I am not what I was in the cold, in the dark.
Neither the joy
before grief, nor the joy after.

Only the inflected
spark at the base of the spine.

Half-conscious spark. Indifferent spasm.

The spill of night into flesh gone nameless,
sliding and flowing
into nothing as real as this pounding of the heart.

from *The Georgia Review*

First Time Reading Freud

◊   ◊   ◊

My copy of his *Introductory Lectures*
had an odor I couldn't place, an organic,
vaguely fleshy . . . pulpy . . . baby wipes–
type smell—though not exactly. At 18
I was having trouble concentrating,
though the words, according to theory
were processing themselves in my unconscious
while I kept track of girls in miniskirts
wafting in and out of Olin Library
like wide-winged tropical birds. I'd glance down
at Freud's bleak head floating on the cover,
half in stark shadow, monocle in place,
then gaze across the room at a Korean beauty
whose virtually flat face had gotten her
some modeling jobs, and covers of her own.
She promised her mother she'd wear pantyhose
every day, to help keep out the boys—
as if we'd get inside by accident.
I put my nose to Freud, bent the spine back
deeper to smell . . . an infant's soft moist head?
. . . a mother's breast dusted with talc?

I learned about the promise to her mother
when I pointed to new packages of hose
stacked tall on a chair by her bed.
I don't know how I got into her room
or how Freud's language crept into my head—
superego, pleasure principle,
displacement, latent and *manifest,*

and all that ugly Oedipus business—
babies with sex and murder on the brain,
little Viennese girls hard-wired
to admire their first glimpse of *zomething egstra,*
yet why hadn't I touched mine till I was 16,
and why did our professor have to tell us
about the woman he saw at Woodstock
lifting her naked baby to manipulate
his penis in her mouth, both mother
and son *cooing,* he said, with pleasure?
Does anybody see a problem here?
he asked an amphitheater full of freshmen.
Manipulate was the verb he used. Spackling
putty—that's what that book smelled like.

from *The New York Quarterly*

Zones

◊   ◊   ◊

There are bootprints on the moon, as permanent
as airlessness provides for; she's seen photographic proof,
their tread an orderly, distinctly human
grid left in the dust . . . and yet she can't influence
Chino's heart just one inch on the other side
of his sternum: and she thumps, as if to prove it,
the chest of her obdurate sixteen-year-old son,
his drugs, his whores, his what-not, while
he stares at her through a mask-of-a-face then
turns away to something more important. Later
I leave, too; I drive back home, eleven city blocks
is a million miles away. Who knows and who knows

and who ever knows? A delivery girl at the airport
with a box, *Hand Carry Only* ★HUMAN EYES★, and
yawning as if she holds a baggie of burgers. Who
believes, at this late date, that any politician's face
betrays a single clue of emotion any more
than gold face-plates of ancient Cretan sea-kings
in a museum case? The light comes down
as probing as it is in a police interrogation room.
The light comes down as tossed, as unreliable, as it is
in a storm-shook linden tree. Spectroscopy: "we know more now
about the composition of the stars than, say, what constitutes
an act of love in the house across the street."

from *Shenandoah*

31

The Fullness Thereof

◊   ◊   ◊

*The earth is the Lord's, and the fullness thereof; the world, and
they that dwell therein.*

—*Psalm 24*

i.

In the beginning a riot of color, burnt umber, magenta,
madder red. Vast expanses of indigo. There was thunder
and the absence of thunder. There was heat, earth shifting,
hills swelling, ridges rising. Then came the fingerlings,
the frogs, and dark-eyed juncos. Possum and hawk
and fox. There were buffalo, mountain lions. There were
slender legs of spiders and dragonflies. Mosquitoes trapped
on salmon-colored salamanders' flickering tongues. Black
bears lumbering through the underbrush. Speckled eggs,
beavers, fire ants. Night crawlers wriggling below, crows
cawing above, there was Earth and the fullness thereof.

ii.

We forded the river, the one named Euphrates, the highest
mountain, we called it Mount George, the one we crossed
over, Mount Spotswood. We numbered the trout and catfish,
the brooks they swam in. We tracked all species of fowl.
We blazed trails in the forest and left distinguishing marks.
The winnowing down of daylight, that was good. Once

two geese swooped in. He swam up and down the pond
fixing his amber eye on me. She tucked her head beneath
one wing. Stars were our faithful companions, and we drank
to their health, as we did to the King and the rest of the Royal
Family. In this way we cleared the path to today.

iii.

It's hard to think of home without the hawthorn and the scat
of deer and mole. It's hard to think of fall without the sight
of scurrying squirrels packing nuts into their cheeks, fearing
humans less than winter. It's hard to think of me without my
hound, my hound, heaven's staunchest ally. It's hard to live
on this land without hearing sounds of all sorts of creatures, all
digging out toward light, or burrowing within, breathing deeply
of the darkening night. To love a place is to love where you are,
to know it is beyond compare, the air, the scent, it might as well
be skin, it is to touch, be touched by everything in the surround,
to feel at one yet fully other in this diverse dominion.

from *The Gettysburg Review*

Definition of Terms

◇   ◇   ◇

Maybe it's because my mother met my father through the kosher butcher,
kosher meaning conforming to stubbornness,
butcher meaning to walk through life with bloody hands,
& me, the bread of this affliction,
leavened with the yeast of insistent immigrant ancestors.

Maybe it's because the night before their wedding, the cracked fortune cookie
warned, "You are doomed to be happy in marriage,"
doomed meaning inevitable guilt,
happy meaning one who is blind to missed opportunity,
the zest of an orange slice eaten from the rind.

Maybe it's because my mother grew up in Weehawken, New Jersey,
land of Lincoln Tunnel & of Aaron Burr's duel,
wee from the Austro-Hungarian meaning trust no one,
hawken from the Lenni Lenape meaning to clear one's throat
before saying nothing important.

Maybe it's because my father had a weak will & a weaker liver,
always flirted with the waitress, "I'll take a Sloe Comfort-able Screw,"
sloe meaning that which is derived from the wild plum,
comfort meaning the satisfaction of longing,
the way the juice hides the hardness of vodka.

Whatever it is, you won't understand when I say our love is like a hammer &
    sickle.
You will look at me with the eyes of your Irish ancestors

while we grind each day into a protective touch of cheek at night.
You will scrub the foundation powder from your face
but will never get rid of the burden that falls in the lines of your skin.

from *Southwest Review*

Eve in the Fall

◊　◊　◊

Summer torn down, petal by petal.
Had the father of storms spent himself at last?
An avalanche of stony silence fell.

And then my eyelids fluttered open
as they had that first morning
I saw you beside me, strangest of creatures,

the one most like me. But this time you were old.
When I looked closer, I saw myself
in your eyes, a fallen leaf starting to curl.

I heard a rustling, insistent,
a tree trying to shake off the past
or a river feeling its way past a wall

toward some vast body of tears
it hadn't known existed. Down the street,
trucks trundled their dark goods

into eternity, one red light after another.
Though it was morning,
street lamps trudged down the sidewalk

like husbands yawning on the way to work.
On puddles, on rags of cloud,
they spilled their weak, human light.

With shadow my cup overflowed.

from *The New Criterion*

The Record

◊　◊　◊

Kisses, too, tasted of iron
the year we lived in twilights. They tilted warily
like bags of groceries I'd carry up the stairs
to find you in boxers, the smell of coffee mixed with vinegar
from the bowl of pickle juice you soaked your fingers in
trying to hurry the callouses. We trafficked in the grief
of incompatible day and night, we stretched the hours
as best we could, but mostly we practiced
a kind of starving, excruciating to recall
how hard we tried. I'd unpack the groceries
and tell you about the day, and after dinner
you'd pick out a tune on the guitar
(it was the year you apprenticed to the blues).
Before each night shift, in uniform and socks,
you'd climb into bed and hold me until I fell asleep.
Then you would slip quietly out.
And when I dreamed, I glimpsed the gods in you,
I dreamt you were Hephaestus with the iron forge,
the sweat covering you when you jogged home
was holy, it was the sweat of the whole city,
even the roses, even the bus exhaust.
The mind circles back like a record spinning,
a little molten, a little wobbly, a record
shiny as your black hair, a record player
crackling and stuttering over a scratch, an urge
to ask forgiveness even though it's dark now
and you've already forgiven me.

from *The Southern Review*

Ode to Airheads, Hairdos, Trains to and from Paris

◊   ◊   ◊

For an hour on the train from Beauvais to *Paris*
        Nord I'm entertained by the conversation of three
American girls about their appointment the next
        day with a hairdresser, and if there is a subtext
to this talk, I'm missing it, though little else. Will bangs
        make them look too dykey? And layers, sometimes they hang
like the fur of a shaggy dog. Streaks, what about blond
        streaks? "Whore," they scream, laughing like a coven of wild
monkeys, and after they have exhausted the present
        tense, they go on to the remembrance of hairdos past—
high school proms, botched perms, late-night drunken cuts. The Loch Ness
        Monster would be lost in their brains as in a vast, starless
sea, but they're happy, will marry, overpopulate
        the Earth, which you can't say about many poets,
I think a few weeks later taking the eighty-four
        bus to the hairdresser, where I'll spend three long hours
and leave with one of the best cuts of my life from Guy,
        who has a scar on his right cheek and is Israeli,
but before that I pass a hotel with a plaque—
        Attila József, great Hungarian poet, black
moods and penniless, lived there ten years before he threw
        himself under a train in Budapest. If we knew
what the years held, would we alter our choices, take the train
        at three-twenty instead of noon, walk in the rain
instead of taking the metro? The time travel films
        I adore speak to this very question: overwhelmed

by disease and war, the future sends Bruce Willis back
    to stop a madman. I could be waiting by the track
as József arrives in Paris, not with love but money,
    which seemed to be the missing ingredient, the honey
he needed to sweeten his tea. Most days I take the B
    line of the RER, and one of the stops is Drancy,
the way station for Jews rounded up by the Nazis
    before being sent in trains to the camps, but we can't see
those black-and-white figures in the Technicolor
    present like ghosts reminding us with their pallor
how dearly our circus of reds and golds has been purchased
    and how in an instant all those colors could be erased.

from *Indiana Review*

The Safe House

◇ ◇ ◇

You don't speak of it, not ever,
But you make sure it's always there:
That remote, delicious contingency, the hold,
The hideout at the end of the narrow, nameless
Lane with no light, the long back road
That twists and forks relentlessly, so that
Unless you know the way, you'll never find it.
Unless your mind happens to work that way,
In which case, not only do you know damn well
How to get there (could walk it blind), you simply
Can't survive without it. A real house (Wood
Frame, Cape), unclaimed in any county
Book of deeds, unmarked on any map,
Unrung by doorbell or by phone.
A space without a title.
Just stop. Just think about that for a second.

Furnished simply: in the first room, a couch,
Two matching lamps, a hotplate, and a well-
Stocked bar; beyond, the bedroom and adjoining
Bath, a closet full of scoop-necked, small-
Waisted satin dresses, a corset, heeled sandals,
Stockings. You don't have to plan beyond that;
In fact, all you really need's the impetus
And means to get there, both of which
Involve a man—two at most—chosen
With great care, of course; so often
They go south, soprano, pull that sucker
Punch on you. But this time, this one's

A pro; he puts it all together, really comes
Through: job (how grand, the larceny!),
Signal, getaway. You just have to wait
For the single playing card (king of diamonds)
To appear beneath the door of your apartment
In the city, or the phone call where it rings
Three times and then stops dead, the last bell's echo
Telling IT'S DONE; It's all come down; You better
Scram; sure enough, there's a guy waiting out back
In a black Packard with no plate, engine running.
You're gone, and then you're there; aloud, alone,
You count the clasps along the corset's lace
(Twelve, a dim attempt to calm) and slip on your best:
The gold satin number that shimmers
In very low light. Just then, in perfect time
There flits that four-note tune, a whistle (jazz riff,
The last note quizzical). He's done away with your
Unfortunate chauffeur and stands, hip-shot,
At the door, looks you down and up, and grins,
"I always told you to think of me as your ace in the hole."

Although the common meaning of the phrase
Is lost on you due to lack of poker experience,
The image of swift penetration swims pleasantly,
Warmly to your mind, as ice cracks in the glass
Of the highball you poured yourself somewhere
Inside, and he puts both hands on your waist,
Presses you firmly against the bulletproof
Wall, grabs the back of your neck and plants
One deep, firm kiss. Sure, it's not that big
A house, but you've belonged to those before,
And always had to run like hell—too much arson,
Strangulation, broken china, and then of course
The coppers, firemen, ambulances, and worse,
All those goddamn neighbors gaping. This one's
Simple, and it's all yours, paid in full, just the right
Combination of terror and sin, and the sheer
Exhilaration of the coupling: flight,
And the man at the end in the dark,
A real deadbolt, strongbox, cipher

(Down the hatch); oh love,
Just let me curl my finger round this latch
And let you in.

from *Painted Bride Quarterly*

Houses

◇   ◇   ◇

They've been around in dreams a long time now,
These houses where nobody lives, hidden
Along long stretches of field, accessible
If you run alone down dirt and gravel roads

Late in the afternoon when shadows start
To sift like sand. I think you'll know the place
Better than I. Maybe you'll finish this poem.
Here's my attempt to hand it over to you:

The time. The place. The sound. They fade from me
As my pen scratches across the ragged page
And the cat lounges, observing every move.
By the time I climb upstairs to sit before

My glowing screen, how many years and days
Will have gone by? But only you will know.
Someone is sitting in an upstairs window,
Head bent beside a desk lamp shining. You knock.

No other houses show. There is no answer.
You cross the dusty living room. A grove
Of alder trees, entwined in vines, appears
Out back—on the mantle, a clock without a face.

The crickets cry their stridulation from
The shade. The nighthawk with its plaintive cry
And rush of wings shows up at the right time.
Nothing stirs upstairs. You look in every room.

The moonlight shines through a far window. Now
The poem begins. The anticipated turn.
The much awaited answer from the trees.
Here is the moment when translation begins.

from *Pleiades*

JIM HARRISON

Sunday Discordancies

◊   ◊   ◊

This morning I seem to hear the nearly inaudible
whining grind of creation similar to the harmonics
of pine trees in the wind. My outrageously lovely
hollyhocks are now collapsing of their own weight,
clearly too big for their britches. I'm making notes
for a novel called "The End of Man, and Not Incidentally,
Women and Children," a fable for our low-living time.
Quite early after walking the dogs, who are frightened
of the Sandhill Cranes in the pasture, I fried some ham
with a fresh peach, a touch of brown sugar and clove.
Pretty good but I was wondering at how the dogs
often pretend the Sandhill Cranes don't exist despite
their mighty squawks, like we can't hear
the crying of coal miners and our wounded in Iraq.
A friend on his deathbed cried and said it felt good.
He was crying because he couldn't eat, a lifelong habit.
My little grandson Silas cried painfully until he was fed
macaroni and cheese and then he was merry indeed.
I'm not up to crying this morning over that pretty girl
in the row boat fifty-five years ago. I heard on the radio
that we creatures have about a billion and a half
heartbeats to use. Voles and birds use theirs fast
as do meth heads and stockbrokers, while whales
and elephants are slower. This morning I'm thinking
of recounting mine to see exactly where I am.
I warn the hummingbirds out front, "just slow down,"
as they chase me away from the falling hollyhocks.

from *Five Points*

DOLORES HAYDEN

Grave Goods

◊   ◊   ◊

Tang dynasty camel, painted earthenware, A.D. 600–900

Life flows in the easy stride and flaring tongue
of the long-necked crying camel whose twin humps
bear man, boy, monkey, dog, puppy, and pig.

The monkey nibbles a plum, the dog lies quiet,
the puppy watches the busy monkey chew,
snout down, the pig snores in the noonday heat

as the camel's pacing hooves step west—Changan,
Dunhuang, Lop Nor, Kashgar, Samarkand.
Behind the driver, the boy sits facing backwards,

riding past all the towns with all the souks
and all the tents he might have lived and died in.
The driver smiles under his wide mustache,

confident in the market for fresh almonds,
fine silk, and lap dogs. Clever foreigner
wearing a pointed cap, he knows the way,

he never tires, he is the perfect conductor,
in his hands the trip to places so remote
begins to seem almost manageable.

And so the *mingqi* sculptor soothed the grief
of the dead boy's relatives, conjuring trade
to entertain and profit him. And as for you,

admiring the wondrous camel here with me,
I dread that swaying seat on the camel's back,
I would hold you by our fireside, if only I could.

from *Southwest Review*

A House Is Not a Home

◊   ◊   ◊

It was the night I embraced Ron's wife a bit too long
because he'd refused to kiss me goodbye
that I realized the essential nature of sound.
When she slapped me across one ear,
and he punched me in the other, I recalled,
almost instantly, the purr of liquor sliding
along the neck of the bottle a few hours earlier
as the three of us took turns imitating the croon
of the recently-deceased Luther Vandross.
I decided then, even as my ears fattened,
to seek employment at the African-American
Acoustic and Audiological Accident Insurance Institute,
where probably there is a whole file devoted
to Luther Vandross. And probably it contains
the phone call he made once to ask a niece
the whereabouts of his very first piano.
I already know there is a difference
between hearing and listening,
but to get the job, I bet I will have to learn
how to transcribe church fires or how to categorize
the dozen or so variations of gasping, one of which
likely includes Ron and me in the eighth grade
the time a neighbor flashed her breasts at us.
That night at Ron's house I believed he, his wife,
and Luther loved me more than anything
I could grasp. "I can't believe you won't kiss me,
you're the gayest man I know!" I told him
just before shackling my arms around his wife.
"My job is all about context," I will tell friends

when they ask. "I love it, though most days
all I do is root through noise like a termite
with a number on his back." What will I steal?
Rain falling on a picket sign, breathy epithets—
you think I'm bullshitting. When you have no music,
everything becomes a form of music. I bet
somewhere in Mississippi there is a skull
that only a sharecropper's daughter can make sing.
I'll steal that sound. More than anything,
I want to work at the African-American
Acoustic and Audiological Accident Insurance Institute
so that I can record the rumors and raucous rhythms
of my people, our jangled history, the slander
in our sugar, the ardor in our anger, a subcategory
of which probably includes the sound particular to one
returning to his feet after a friend has knocked him down.

from *Callaloo*

The Way of All the Earth

◇   ◇   ◇

Joshua 23:14

In various ways we'll be taken. Fine, except
that we know it, and just when we've tricked it away
someone nearby—a sister, say, or a child—proves it again

as fact. More pleasant to be one of those turtles
who each September takes a last breath
and goes gliding down to the profound

mud to wag in for a fine six months
of anti-meditation. How brown it would be,
and more than milky, an opaque shell

around the shell of the body, any minnow who passed
taking the body for rocks that had sat on the bottom
for centuries, mossing. We would not attend

the last rites of our families. We would be happy
as stone until spring when we swam upwards
to catch ducks in our snappers—

oh, unavoidable affront, especially
for the old, for whom death's quick mouth
darts daily through reed and shallow pool.

It snatches from the surface the children
and sleek teens of the past, each month a volley
of funerals, leading up to the snap over a webbed foot,

when the self, which quakes and rages, is dragged under
until it is drowned. Better, perhaps, not to go
alone, but to pile, instead, like other turtles

on top of one another in a river's trench—
to stay alive by being nearly dead. When the winter of dust
blustered and whirled sixty-four million years back,

and the great beasts who stalked the land suffered
and fell, their bulk heaving the hills—
all of that was only a loud game of billiards

to the turtles, who sank down away from the light
and let the arms and legs float in the waters,
each belly atop another shell, the skin assuming

the work of the lungs, so the lungs—
as the earth above wasted and tore—
might, through that din, be still.

from *The Antioch Review*

Mum's the word

◊   ◊   ◊

The Depression wasn't a good time
for birthday cakes. Whatever was around
sufficed. In '37 it was an onion, then potato
bugs, everyone passed on the three-layer cake
of gravel. You're seventy-five today,
you can have any cake you want.
With seven kids, a cake of stretch marks
seems right. Eat what time
has done to you. Cake of bad heart.
Of husband love. If getting older's
a test, reaching one hundred's
an A+. I give you, Mom, a solid C. Time's wingéd
defibrillator. I've never asked how old
you feel you are in your pineal gland,
my soulimage is seventeen, he runs and runs
on liquid legs. For talking purposes,
say you're eight in the mirror
of how you see yourself, a veritable punk,
so of course you'll die young.
I'm right behind you if it helps
in trusting the afterlife's not my problem.
Say we become static on the AM dial.
Say we wear the silly hats of popes.
Say the slogan of eternity is "One Size
Fits All." There's something after this,
even if that something is nothing,
just as, when you were a kid, the words
"you're it" made the person it, and whatever
it was, you chased it, didn't you, all afternoon

for years, until dusk told you
the trees were getting sleepy. Soon
you were in your pajamas, sticking your arm
out the window into the night, wondering
if your hand would come back, it did and will
every time but once.

from *The Georgia Review*

A Democratic Vista

◇   ◇   ◇

The poets were speaking at the Symposium
On Poetry and the National Purpose, attended
By many in the crowd, many poets and lovers
Of poetry and many lovers of poets
While one of the poets, the one I'll call
The Poet, was telling the crowd, especially
The members thereof who themselves were in fact
Not poets, that nothing is as significant as Poets,
For it is poets who are the prophets of the race
As well as its annalists, yes, its analysts who notice not
Only what has happened and is happening to the race
But announce beforehand what is going to happen
—And that isn't all; they make it happen,
They change your lives—while, as I say, The Poet
Was saying all this and the crowded crowd
Was brought to the verge of cheers while
He was chanting the terrific openness of the ego
Like a continent uncontained by the roiling steel
Breakers of any sea, he celebrates the openness
Of the great variety counter as plenitudinous as appetites,
Making of everything the ingredients for a possible
Though unexampled ingestion whether of delight
Disgust or what for others would be terror
Like the knowledge of his own death
Which becomes only one layer in his hero sandwich
Surrounded with relish by the cries of the suffering
The outcasts the whores the battle-losers
And the captains of wrecked ships all
Equally in the feast and of the feast and

At the feast with the color green the shouts
Of victors and the amorous bodies
Of young men—you might not think so but it proved
That this unmetered and immeasurable readiness
To keep from being fenced in by anything by being
The self that does the including excluding
Nothing but tragedy—this, this is the American
Way. The Camerado for whom he waits at the end
Of the long road, *c'est nous,* the children spawned in the open
Nets of his liberties. Between his long spiels
It's we who pick up our tickets at the Thruway
Tollbooths, erect new shopping centers in the interstices
Of his strophes to the future, growing older while his leaves
Rattle in the wind. We turn the page to see his
Democratic Vista—"Never was there more
Hollowness of heart . . . the underlying principles
Of the States are not honestly believed in
Nor is humanity itself believed in," he told us before
A century and a half brought us to the future
He believed in, saying, "I know nothing grander,
More positive proof of the past, the triumphant
Result of faith in human-kind than a well-contested
American national election," a sentiment we
Perhaps had better leave Open-
                                    ended—

                   from *The New Criterion*

RICHARD   HOWARD

Arthur Englander's Back in School

◊   ◊   ◊

Dear Mrs Masters, as you probably know,
almost half our Fifth Grade Class is Jewish—not
      a majority
but *lots,* without even counting our teacher
Miss Husband, who's getting married (next June) to
      a *gentile husband*!
—that has to change more than her name, doesn't it?
Well, your office records must show who's really
      Jewish and who's not,
and for some of us who just *happen* to be
Jewish, those records might be the only sure
      indication of
our race or faith or whatever makes us Jews,
and therefore different from the other kids
      (no one really knows).
But this week our Rabbi told us this weird thing:
he says there are Jews—mostly in Hasidic
      congregations and
they're mostly in Brooklyn—who perform (between
Rosh Hashana and Yom Kippur) this ritual
      called *pekkarot*—no,
that's backward, the Hebrew word is *kapparot*—
during which Believers swing a live chicken
      high over their heads:
this whirling is meant to transfer the Hasid's
sins to the chicken, which is then sacrificed.
      Rabbi Abraham

57

said about 50,000 chickens are used
in ceremonies all over Brooklyn—
                    that's a lot of birds
to get slaughtered (after being whirled), and most
wind up in someone's pot. Not everyone whirls
            chickens, there are some
Orthodox Believers who whirl money instead—
Maimonides himself once called *kapparot*
                a pagan practice
that should be abandoned, but our Rabbi says
it's going strong in Brooklyn and can't be stopped.
            Now Mrs Masters,
we've learned—trust Duncan Chu to find out, of course—
that Arthur Englander's late parents
                were Hasidic Jews
(Arthur was the boy who killed that peacock, but
you wouldn't punish him, even though we voted
            unanimously
to expel him from the Fifth Grade), and when we
went to see his Aunt, she showed us a photo
                of Arthur, age six,
wearing gloves and whirling a big white rooster
for *kapparot* . . . No one knew where he had gone
            after What Happened,
but you said we should help him "find himself"
if he came back to Park School, and of course
                the police found him
right away. Mrs Masters, we think Arthur
believed he had to slaughter that poor peacock
            for his *kapparot*—
he got it all mixed up with vampire movies
and that's what he meant when he screamed
                he had to do it
right. Christine Rath says that's how religions work.
Even when we've forgotten what they mean
            we do what we think
are the same things people have always done.
But we forget. Or we change. And Christine's
                not even Jewish!
And then Duncan Chu said that religions die

once they're proved to be true. And that Science is
          the tombstone of dead
religions. And Duncan's not Jewish either.
But David Stashower is, so he had to
                    tell what his father
thinks: that Scientists now say the same thing
as Rabbis, but without capital letters.
          Arthur Englander
paid no attention to what anyone had said,
but now most of us want him back in Fifth Grade
                    with all the others.

          from *The New Republic*

In Winter

◊   ◊   ◊

> *Let the crookedness and straightness*
> *bespeak the light.*
> —Allen Ginsberg, "Psalm III"

I know the crooked at once. How it tries
to circle, catch a sudden pale gleam,
how it sparks a pearly surprise
against the sky, its silhouette
making a little bend

just before the sun is visible. The straight
is harder. No curves, no beckoning,
just unendingly in the place

we're used to. It's not exactly
boring. It can stiffen hard to flatten
silence in the light while it seeks.
Maybe that's why looking for light
when the season says *Hanukkah*

is hard and easy: the Maccabees fight,
win, the Greek Syrians leave—the straight plain
facts plus one drop of oil burning
for eight days to light up
the crooked and the casual, just for kids.

Maybe light, plain light
is always unexpected, like a trick?

When we stand in the yard
at night, we see the stars window-
gleam at us, as though really
we can hold on to them inside,
behind the glass.

This morning before the sun
could struggle through the fog, we found
a dead bluebird on our deck.
It stayed so long in the garden

this fall we could watch it flicker
blue light up and down
through all the evergreens.

Did the window glass play a trick
on the bluebird, some blaze
of enlightenment it knew
it had to reach? It's so hard
to fling yourself against a mirage
in the dark. Each year
when *Hanukkah* makes winter official

we'll remember
the straight blue wings
lying flat, think of the surprisingly
crooked pearly legs catching
a sparkle, wavering up
in two skinny half-circles

in the fog as if they had
a kind of faith
in the continuing light.

from *Calyx*

How to Be Eaten
by a Lion

◊   ◊   ◊

—*for Claire Davis*

If you hear the rush, the swish of mottled sand
and dust kicked up under the striving paws,
its cessation, falling into the sharp and brittle grass
like the tick of a tin roof under sun
or hint of rain that nightly wakes you,
try to stand your ground. Try not to scream,
for it devalues you. That tawny head and burled
mange, the flattened ears of its sleek engine
will seem only a blur, a shock, a shadow
across your neck that leaves you cold.
It may seem soft, barely a blow,
more like a falling, an exquisite giving
of yourself to the ground, made numb
by those eyes. It may be easier just to watch,
for fighting will only prolong things,
and you will have no time to notice the sky,
the texture of dust, what incredible leaves
the trees have. Instead, focus on your life,
its crimson liquor he grows drunk on.
Notice the way the red highlights his face,
how the snub nose is softened, the lips made
fuller; notice his deft musculature, his rapture,
because in all of creation there is not art
to compare with such elegance, such simplicity.

Notice this and remember it,
this way in which you became beautiful
when you thought there was nothing more.

from *Mid-American Review*

To Yahweh

◊   ◊   ◊

*"YHWH is definitely a verb form. We can take comfort in the
certain knowledge that God is a verb, not a noun or an adjective."*
—*The Gifts of the Jews,* Thomas Cahill

God is the spray on your lip from the freshly poured ginger ale.
No, God is the arrival on your lip of the spray. The arcing. The spree.

God is definitely not that weird sexuality of wild bird rehabilitators.
God is, instead, waves blown back hard from the shore. At night.

Perhaps he is the rumbling scaring done by the haunted freight train,
the shrill ghouls in the back cars climbing over each other to escape.

God is weequashing: The spearing of eels or fish from a canoe by torchlight.
God is the inventing of words like *weequashing.*

She is not the fire darkening down.
She is the goldfinch singing the whisper song.

And the birthing of a second child, to feel your body blooming.
To feel head, then shoulders, thighs then cord tumbling. To live. To life!

To give the initial downbeat to the tympanis. To cure mice by placing them
in a cello.
To do whatever the scarecrow did with his brains. And to make that *acrid
or burned quality*

of the smell of space. To crow, to fly, to gild and gnaw. To mean. Shape, shear, smear and shine. Play and improvise. To last.

from *Southwest Review*

MAUD KELLY

What I Think of Death, If Anyone's Asking

◊   ◊   ◊

Let me tell you about the cows, how scientists driven
by some dark need to see them digest, really see it,
cut holes in the sides of twenty and inserted glass
ringed with plastic there, riveted it to their skin,
creating in each a porthole, so that when they stood
together, sleepily chewing, at the icy edge of a Missouri
sunrise they looked not unlike a fleet of cow ships, moored
illogically to a barn, bobbing on a sea of frozen sod.

Let me tell you how I stumbled, nineteen and drunk,
across a field to touch one on a dare—*the window,*
the boy had hissed, shoving the bottle at me
for one last drink, *it has to be the window*—
how I moved, stubbing my feet, shivering woozy,
eyes half-mooned from groping, and was almost there,
hoping the boy was watching, impressed
and aroused, his eyes blazing with the joke of it all,
how, then, from nowhere and all at once the long arm
of time's elliptical arc swooped in, wrapped me
in its cello-thin line, how I stopped, looked at the cows,
wondered what they must see coming toward them,
what monster upon them now, mad with curiosity
and no doubt a map of what to peel back next,
having already torn open and plexiglassed
their stomachs, would it be their hearts, or would I take

their souls, undo the papery layers of their thoughts,
pull the thread of their breath to unravel the tones of their lowing.

I am telling you how I reached the point I always knew
would come, when I was at once too old and far
too young, how I knew, really knew for the first time
that there's a wildness in us, how that made me sick
but I couldn't go back, so I went toward the only cow
who watched not me but the sun, pink as a newborn,
heaving itself through the trees. I went to her, leaned
my head on her back, the sun growing, the boy
turning, her belly reflecting the last of the stars.

from *American Literary Review*

Why do you keep putting animals in your poems?

◊   ◊   ◊

I open windows to catch a glimpse of *grace*
on the horizon, and in they sneak, coyotes and crows,
pikas and the scholarly vole, dragging scoured skies
I can see myself in. Much cheaper than booking
a flight to the Galápagos. And they teach me.

Badgers rarely invent stories to make them sad
about their bodies. And the wrinkliest of Shar Peis
never dreams of ironing its face. My happiness
is like a flock of sparrows that scatters when a bus
drives by, then re-strings itself two blocks away,

a necklace of chirps festooning a caved-in barn.
Capuchin monkeys will bite a millipede to release
a narcotic toxin, then pass the millipede to a neighbor
as if it were a joint at a concert. In a Rhode Island
nursing home, Oscar the miracle cat curls up

with residents hours before they expire, converting
death into purrs for the next world. A poem is grave
and nursery: the more creatures you bury in one place,
the more hunger bursts forth somewhere else,
like bats at Carlsbad when the brightest day turns dark.

The night I stood on my sister's feet and learned
to waltz, a porcupine braved four lanes of asphalt

and hurtling machines to chomp our windfall apples—
two miracles of syncopation held together by a harvest
moon. As Marianne Moore taught us, an hour

at the Bronx Zoo in a tricorn hat leaves one happier
than nine months with a shrink. Comes a time
you just have to wiggle your pin feathers,
wag your ghost tail, feel your teeth grow long
for the ragged salmon throwing their bodies upstream.

from *Indiana Review*

Open Field

◇　◇　◇

Forget the comma, the crow said, darting
onto another branch, random joy being his,

being mine, being yours, depending on how
you look at a branch, which is, after all,

something essential for him, for you, for me,
his wings no more no less than the wings

of his fellow travelers, his curious, forlorn
pecking at what—a pecking for what is new.

And isn't that what we want, to be taken
out of a sentence into the air, where conversation

blossoms into speechlessness, the bosom
of belonging, being in rather than on, in being here.

But the comma said, how dare you abandon
the curl that tells how distinctly different

one iota is from another, lifting a note a little
higher or lower, casting a shadow over whatever

may follow, or making a sudden clearing
for the future, letting it tremble, hesitate, sing,

announcing how each thing depends on another,
touching, resting, going on, dying and ferreting

too, yes, that too, did you think it impossible to do
another thing after arriving, did you forget the

moment awakening after a dark dry dot,
that jab of ending, a minuscule well sounding

no less no more than a drop of the sap
asleep in winter trees, did you believe for a split

second you could breeze on by or pass
such a point without calling out to its source?

O, said the crow,
but didn't you know:

I
am a drop

of the bottomless well,
you are a mark in the snow.

from *The Kenyon Review*

Words on the Wind

◊   ◊   ◊

—Ford River Rouge

I'd walk up the hill through wild grasses
rich with milkweed and flags and make a nest
in the place I'd tamped down over the days
of decent weather. The view was something
terrifying and never the same:
on calm days the great plumes rose straight up
to insult the delicate nostrils of angels.
I was twenty-four and had no use
for the God of my fathers, no use for any-
thing spiritual. I believed in the deepest organs,
the liver, the kidneys, the heart, the lungs.
Nonetheless as I sat cross-legged drinking
chocolate milk words came on the wind.
Can you imagine God speaking to you
as you ate a little round store-bought pie
on a hilltop in Dearborn, where no Jews
were welcomed, where the wind came
in waves through the wild grasses
that had the guts to thrive? How I yearned
for the character of weeds and grass
that seemed more mysterious and grand
than the words the wind scattered through air
so fetid it was sweet. Noon, May 12,
1952. I wrote it on a calendar
at home and later threw the thing away.
You want those words, you who still believe,
who think the exact words are essential

to your salvation or whatever
it is you pray for? I'll take you there
on a spring day of wind and low gray sky,
a Dearborn day. We'll bring two quarts
of chocolate milk and little store-bought
pies—apple, cherry, or pineapple,
each worse than the other—and find the nest
of fifty years ago, and maybe we'll smoke
as all young men did, and lean back
into the flattened grass, and rest our heads
on the cold ground while we add our own
exhalations to the exquisite chaos
of the air, and commune with whomever.

from *The Georgia Review*

Tell the Bees

◇   ◇   ◇

Tell the bees. They require news of the house;
they must know, lest they sicken
from the gap between their ignorance and our grief.
Speak in a whisper. Tie a black swatch
to a stick and attach the stick to their hive.
From the fortress of casseroles and desserts
built in the kitchen these past few weeks
as though hunger were the enemy, remove
a slice of cake and lay it where they can
slowly draw it in, making a mournful sound.

And tell the fly that has knocked on the window all day.
Tell the redbird that rammed the glass from outside
and stands too dazed to go. Tell the grass,
though it's already guessed, and the ground clenched in furrows;
tell the water you spill on the ground,
then all the water will know.
And the last shrunken pearl of snow in its hiding place.

Tell the blighted elms, and the young oaks we plant instead.
The water bug, while it scribbles
a hundred lines that dissolve behind it.
The lichen, while it etches deeper
its single rune. The boulders, letting their fissures widen,
the pebbles, which have no more to lose,
the hills—they will be slightly smaller, as always,

when the bees fly out tomorrow to look for sweetness
and find their way
because nothing else has changed.

from *Poetry*

The Happy Majority

◊　◊　◊

. . . before I join the great and, I believe, the happy majority.
—P. T. Barnum

Before I join the happy majority (though I doubt one member happy
or unhappy) I have some plans: to discover several new species
of beetle; to jump from a 100-foot platform
into a pile—big enough
to break my fall—of multicolored lingerie;
to build a little heater
(oh not to join the happy ones,
until some tasks are done)
beside each tulip bulb to speed its bloom;
to read 42,007 books (list available
on request); to learn to read and/or write
Chinese, CAT scans, Sanskrit, petroglyphs,
and English; to catch a bigot
(oh not to join the happy ones,
until some tasks are done)
by the toe; to kiss
the clavicle of (name available
on request); to pay my respects, again,
at the grave of John Keats; to abrogate
my position in God's nihilistic
(oh not to join the happy ones,
until some tasks are done)
dream; to hold my mother's hand as she leaves this world;
to lay my hand upon my father's heart as he does likewise;

and for my daughter to be glad I was her father as I exit, also
(in a hundred years or so), from the conscious to the un-.

from *The American Poetry Review*

Boarding:
Hemaris thysbe

◇   ◇   ◇

Most large sphinxes pay quiet visits at night,
but not the Hummingbird Clearwing. Black antennae
clamped to its head like forceps, crawling undone
from a bed of thorns, this flying hypodermic is not
what one expects. Its thorax, ridged with green fur,
the base of a light bulb screwed to a lick of fire,
no bird: an imposter, a thumb-sized sea lion with wings
of burnt newspaper, now dousing itself in a milkweed.
And when it unfurls the primal eel of its tongue, longer
than law, long as the lion-moth itself, to wade
what one had thought was a rose, one would surrender
one's timid original hand, let this tongue rinse
away such useless placenta that is *oneself* and not
moth or salt or claw or shadow or heat—

because Pyramus and Thisbe weren't ready for what
they saw. Having forsook their wall for a time
they imagined would be real, with unmodified moonlight
refracting off another's suddenly atomic
face: who can tell the blood from the berry,
the knife from the tooth? Immersed in the brine
of what one desires, a discriminating brain is useless. The peri-
meter shot, the wall rubble, one meets a brand-
new loneliness, alienation without borderlines,
an indifferent, customless sea, where one drowns.
The moth: its umbilical tongue retracts, coils a rung

in its brain. Having peeled the rind off enough suns
for one hour, its wings' alchemical thunder gears
up for today's exit. Yet those antennae, that deliverance:

two black oars angle up from the waves, and the oarsman waits.

from *The American Scholar*

Sweat

◇ ◇ ◇

I think it's gross when girls sweat
—Overheard at the gym

And it's true, the body
    is gross, pungent, flushed
and leaving as it lifts away

    from itself a sticky netting of salt,
crystals seasoning the skin.
    And it's true,

I am gross. Because I want
    this. I want this
brine, this vellum

    of slog, this becoming
barnyard, silk ribbon tanned
    to leather. I grit

my teeth and open
    my throat. Enough
of careful diction, the ulcerative clot

    of deliberation and poise, the crossed
knees and tidy shirtlines, all tied
    up in knots and fists. I've been holding

my past like a buoy. Like an anchor.
　　　Enough. I want this flood, this wash
of chemicals, the ugly glaze

　　　that coats and comes clean.
I want to take my hurt
　　　　like a vitamin, and then

I will let it, *make* it
　　　spirit away. Again and again,
every day, enough water

　　　to drown, except I don't,
because there are a million
　　　invisible exit points.

　　　　from *Cimarron Review*

Canis

◇　◇　◇

It was a small comment, wasn't it, about who they were—
that last year on the dunes when all the talk
was of coyotes, prairie wolf in search of an ocean,

pestilence lurking just over the next hillock,
their footprints instead of rabbits surrounding the shack
each morning or half-sunk in the cranberry bog

just off the path. They heard the howling somewhere
behind their backs as they walked out past midnight
from town, singing at the top of their lungs:

abandon me, oh careless love—though they knew
the coyotes knew exactly where they were. It did not surprise
either of them when the coyotes wailed unusually close

and loud on a moonless night after an argument,
this time a mean one about the dogs. For God's sake,
the dogs, and how much trouble they were

to him, their feeding and whining and constant
need to go out, no matter how wet or cold. And so on
till silence set itself between them, holding stiff

as each turned away to bed. But the coyotes just outside
started up their merciless lament, as if
the entire genus called them, had bound the tribe together

in protest for their brothers. This keening went on for hours,
both of them miserable, sleepless, that rising, falling
complaint in their ears—until he couldn't bear it,

he said I'm sorry, I can't do this anymore, and she in a rush
of understanding the exact suffering fit of it, jumped up
and closed the offending one window

open a half-inch crack, and just like that
the coyotes stopped their noise
in the dead center of a howl; what I mean to say is

the wind stopped making that heartbroken sound.

from *Provincetown Arts*

Lingering Doubts

◇   ◇   ◇

1.

The honeybees dance and are understood,
But their point is always and only nectar.
Achilles spoke with the gods, and all
They wanted was his spear through Hector.

2.

By the Senate's decree, in the heart of Rome
No ominous soldiers were allowed
Except in hollow triumphs where,
More than the general, plated and proud,
The whispering slave amused the crowd.

3.

From pre-hab to re-tox in under a year,
The cynic had run his terror to ground.
The man in the mirror was merely glass.
The world was just "Another round."

4.

The woman giving birth
Was standing near the bed,

The child apparently worth
The risk that lay ahead.
"Don't be stubborn. Here,
Lie down," he crossly said.
She winced and shook her head.
"Spoken just like a man.
Lie down? A bed? That's where
The trouble first began."

5.

The day he left, he said I knew the reason.
Look at the trees. Love only lasts a season.
For years since then, I've stared at them and seen
Only their blackened branches beneath the green.

from *Parnassus*

The Silence
of the Mine Canaries

◊   ◊   ◊

The bats have not flowered
for years now in the crevice
of the tower wall when the long twilight
of spring has seeped across it
as the west light brought back
the colors of parting
the furred buds have not hung there
waking among their dark petals
before sailing out blind along their own echoes
whose high infallible cadenzas only
they could hear completely and could ride
to take over at that hour
from the swallows gliding
ever since daybreak over the garden
from their nests under the eaves
skimming above the house and the hillside pastures
their voices glittering in their exalted tongue
who knows how long now since they have been seen
and the robins have gone from the barn
where the cows spent the summer days
though they stayed long after the cows were gone
the flocks of five kinds of tits have not come again
the blue tits that nested each year
in the wall where their young
could be heard deep in the stones by the window
calling Here Here have not returned
the marks of their feet are still there on the stone

of their doorsill that does not know
what it is missing
the cuckoo has not been heard
again this May
nor for many a year the nightjar
nor the mistle thrush song thrush whitethroat
the blackcap that instructed Mendelssohn
I have seen them
I have stood and listened
I was young
they were singing of youth
not knowing that they were singing for us

from *Alaska Quarterly Review*

The Insect Collector's Demise

◊   ◊   ◊

On mornings free of cloud the insects
mistake my windows for clean platters
of sky and knock against them, seeking entry.

Some make hardly a sound—a sand grain
blown against glass; but others—butterflies,
for instance, kiss a bit harder and leave behind

a whiplash of dust. The mind is a jailer
whose job it is to wake us
when we are not sleeping and I

am suddenly the child I used
to be, running amuck through the garden
with my killing jars and my nets; a child

so in love with the world that she carried
pieces of it everywhere so she would never forget.
There was nothing beautiful

in such dying, in such bluster and panic. My net
had a mesh as soft as a stocking and it held
the scent of chemicals and breakage—a bitterness

like tarnished metal. Every day
there were items left behind—torn wings
like scraps of propaganda, the leg

of a cricket like a dropped hat pin. Forget
formaldehyde and ethyl acetate, forget
the suspect, precarious terrains

into which all collectors go
for a rare specimen; imagine what happens
to a child in that moment

when the matte-black pin, thin as a horse hair,
breaches a cricket's lacquered façade and passes
smoothly, and without resistance, through

the body beneath. In the killing jar,
the crickets were the worst of all—their leaps
against the glass the music

of someone fiddling with the small change
in his pocket. What hubris
to think the insects loved their lives

less than I loved mine. Each one
a verb snatched from the world's mouth.
This is how I grew afraid of details, of all

the precisions of suffering and fell in love
with landscapes viewed from a distance, where
it was everything I could not see

that saved me; where, if there were animals,
they were small and clean on the earth's
green manicure: sunlight washing like varnish

over the backs of black cattle in the fields; sheep,
falling to their knees to get closer
to the sweetest, lower stems of the grass.

And being rewarded. From a distance
each tree was a green trawl of light.
Too far away to hear the leaves' sad

fricative or every tiny murder
in the dirt, this was a world
in which even the hooves and the teeth

of the horses grazing under the eaves of an oak
had never once hurt the grasses; there were
no blast zones of pewter feathers,

no flusters of corruption or scandal
on the leaves' plain crockery;
no ticks dug-in between the jackdaw's

feathers, not a single moth like a banner
in the jaws of an ant. Not a single ant
in a blackbird's beak. At the end

of every trouble, I thought, were fields
like this, fields like sunlit platforms.
God's failed attempts at imagining paradise.

It was everywhere I wasn't: I could step
right into it and never arrive;
and it was always behind me, where the grass

had already shrugged off
the dark kiss of my small boots.
And before me the wrestle of the river,

all purpose and no wastage, and I could feel
the trout's perfect fit within it
where the current grew snug on the inside curve.

> I have wasted my life trying to enter this promise.
> I will waste whatever life I have left.
> In the inch-deep darkness of a tree's body, the egg

of the ichneumon, that persuasive burglar, lies
next to the egg of the wood wasp.
What the world gives, the world

then takes away.

from *The Missouri Review*

Self-Exam

◇　◇　◇

They tell you it won't make much sense, at first,
you will have to learn the terrain. They tell you this
at thirty, and fifty, and some are late
beginners, at last lying down and walking
the old earth of the breasts—the small,
cobbled, plowed field of one,
with a listening walking, and then the other—
fingertip-stepping, divining, north
to south, east to west, sectioning
the little fallen hills, sweeping
for mines. And the matter feels primordial,
unimaginable—dense,
cystic, phthistic, each breast like the innards
of a cell, its contents shifting and changing,
streambed gravel under walking feet, it
seems almost unpicturable, not
immemorial, but nearly un-
memorizable, but one marches,
slowly, through grave or fatal danger,
or no danger, one feels around in the
two tack-room drawers, ribs and
knots like leather bridles and plaited
harnesses and bits and reins,
one runs one's hands through the mortal tackle
in a jumble, in the dark, indoors. Outside—
night, in which these glossy ones were
ridden to a froth of starlight, bareback.

from *The New Yorker*

Red

◇   ◇   · ◇

All the while
I was teaching
in the state of Virginia
I wanted to see
gray fox.
Finally I found him.
He was in the highway.
He was singing
his death song.
I picked him up
and carried him
into a field
while the cars kept coming.
He showed me
how he could ripple
how he could bleed.
Goodbye I said
to the light of his eye
as the cars went by.
Two mornings later
I found the other.
She was in the highway.
She was singing
her death song.
I picked her up
and carried her
into the field
where she rippled
half of her gray

half of her red
while the cars kept coming.
While the cars kept coming.
Gray fox and gray fox.
Red, red, red.

from *Five Points*

LINDA PASTAN

Insomnia

◊   ◊   ◊

I remember when my body
was a friend,

when sleep like a good dog
came when summoned.

The door to the future
had not started to shut,

and lying on my back
between cold sheets

did not feel
like a rehearsal.

Now what light is left
comes up—a stain in the east,

and sleep, reluctant
as a busy doctor,

gives me a little
of its time.

from *The Virginia Quarterly Review*

On Mercy

◊   ◊   ◊

Knowing he was soon to be executed
the condemned man asked if first he might

please
have something to drink, if first he might
be drunk.

So the soldiers brought him a drink
and because there was no hurry, another,
and one for each of them, too.

Soon they were all
very drunk, and this was merciful
because the man probably didn't understand
when they put him to the wall

and shot him.

+

I'll marry the man who can prove this happened,
the dying leaves said

in their descent.

I'll marry the man who looks through that window,
the waiting grasstips said.

But the sun went on with its golden rays
like a zealous child

and the camera-eyed bees jittered mercifully
in the distant branches.

+

The man slept on the floor
and the little mouse in his head also slept.

The soldiers didn't know who would drag him away
or where they should hide him
so they laughed nervously and one
offered the body a drink, *Ha ha,*
                              a toast!

then left him by the rich lady's liquor cabinet
where she'd find him when she returned from the hills.

+

I'll marry the girl who kisses the lips
and brings a breath to them,
the starving horses said from their fields.

I'll marry the man who pounds the chest
and starts the heart,
                    the caved-in houses said.

And the window let the light in
until the sun failed in the branches
and, like mercy,
                    darkness smothered the town.

+

Later in the story, her grown son wrapped him
in a parachute
                    and dumped him in a neighbor's yard.

Later, that neighbor, who understood bad luck,
dragged the man to another's lawn.

And so he traveled, yard-to-yard,
                                        to the edge of town
where at last he slept by a little-traveled road
in a merciful ditch

while bombers unzipped the sky.

+

And when the town burned, he missed it,
and when the treetops bloomed and charred, he missed it.

I'll marry the man,
the grasstips said in the hot wind,

I'll marry the girl,
the horses said, running from their burning barn, aflame,

their bodies glowing bluely in the dusk.

+

And no one proved it happened,
which was merciful for us all,

the road forgotten, the man gone to root and weed,
to marrow and tooth.

+

And if it had—
                    Who would find his jawbone in the loam?
Who would pick out his bullet shells and fillings,
like glitter in the new wood?

And if a man should string them
like words on a golden chain

and make from them a charm,
                            and give them to his wife,
wouldn't that be mercy, too?

from *Field*

Pickled Heads:
St. Petersburg

◊   ◊   ◊

For years they floated in adjacent jars,
   two heads on a dusty storage shelf,
abandoned in a back room of the palace:
   Mary Hamilton and Charles Mons.

We want to make things last. Salt, sugar, sun
   will work, and tannin from chestnut bark, and brains
spread on the skins that toted them, and sometimes
   words. But new two hundred years ago—

these "spirits of wine." (Fermenting's nature, but
   distilling's art.) Not all steam is water,
just as not all passion's love. Boil wine,
   catch what evaporates, trap that alcohol

and it preserves whatever you drop in,
   the head of your wife's lover, for example—
Peter ordered his queen to display it on her mantle—
   or your mistress, killed for infanticide.

They say Great Peter kissed the dead head's lips.
   The bodies sinned, the heads were saved. Don't be
distracted by stories of Joaquin Murrieta
   glaring in a jar in California.

Though he was gunned down by someone named Love,
    his problems were political, not erotic.
He really should remind you of Evita,
    beautifully embalmed, better than Lenin,

then passed around, hot political potato,
    hidden in attics, propped like a doll behind
a movie screen for weeks, deaths unfurling behind her
    like a red scarf from Isadora's car.

And even if Jeremy Bentham's head was found
    once in a luggage locker in Aberdeen,
once in the front quadrangle being used
    as a football by medical students, he died

a natural death and landed in that cabinet,
    stuffed, propped, dressed, through his own will,
wax head on his shoulders, catastrophe in the drawer,
    still convinced Utility was his goal.

The uses the dead are put to by the living.
    Peter saved one for hatred, one for love,
and they outlasted hatred, love, and Peter
    to become flip sides of Death's two-headed coin.

Heads win. Maybe the story
    isn't the heads but Peter, unstoppable
monster consuming youth, a Minotaur
    trapped in the labyrinth he built himself.

Finally Catherine freed them. After decades
    she found them, observed how well their youth and beauty
were preserved, and had them buried, though no one says
    whether bottled or free to stop being beautiful.

from *Prairie Schooner*

Turn

◊   ◊   ◊

The sky then was stapled shut,
the day worming toward gray.
I was walking through brown leaves,
but this isn't about color.
It's about the flat curve of spine
I found in the grass, an arch of coyote
or maybe dog, about the one vertebra
I brought home as a keepsake.

And today my cat wants her chin rubbed
so badly she's fallen off the chair,
made a fool of herself
in front of me out of need—
like the man who moved to town
but found no one would love him
for fixing the rickety house he bought.
Even though it was an eyesore,
even though we all thought
it was a good idea.
But forget his fussy balconies,
his gazebo and lattices and pink roses,
forget our petty city council,
the voluptuousness of government,
the new appraisal he wouldn't pay
hand-delivered by the cops.

This isn't about the lies boys told
or didn't tell reporters, the way he did
or didn't put his hands down their jeans,

or the crowbar he took to his windows, then,
or some hatred I feel for the small towns
I've lived in. People all over the world
make lives in small places, load their donkeys,
wear their hats, cross the river to market
and back. But forget the donkey,
the air full of implosion, the Bible verses
he sprayed red and black on the siding:
"Give them sorrow of heart,
         oh Lord, Thy curse unto them."
"Let death seize upon them
         and let them go down quick into HELL
         for wickedness is in their dwellings."
"God (B)less America."

This isn't about the absolute angles of our streets,
the maps small towns are always misplaced on,
or our big spring tulip festival,
or the holes we dig the way our fathers dug them,
or the way we crawl into them.
This is about the last, red words
we wrung from him, the confession
blotched on the alley side of the house:
"I am not a queer. I am not a faggot"—
when faggot is just the broken end
of a string, a lump, a bundle.
And queer is the twist in us, the turn,
the oblique torch we light and lift
like a lamp beside the open door.

Think of the bone I found as a representative
of all bones, a congress of one.
No matter which way I set it on my desk
a face looks out: the Lone Ranger's,
a buffalo's, a Spanish pilgrim's
under a wide-brimmed hat,
a prize fighter's, a dog's,
a one-eared rat's, an ascendant angel's.
He wanted to be a citizen among strangers.
But this isn't about democracy,

it's about the open oh of the spine
that is who we are: a little story
of armor and ego, a little thread
strung through a few beads.

from *The Journal*

Tonight No Poetry Will Serve

◊   ◊   ◊

Saw you walking barefoot
taking a long look
at the new moon's eyelid

later spread
sleep-fallen, naked in your dark hair
asleep but not oblivious
of the unslept unsleeping
elsewhere

Tonight I think
no poetry
will serve

Syntax of rendition:

verb pilots the plane
adverb modifies action

verb force-feeds noun
submerges the subject
noun is choking
verb   disgraced   goes on doing

there are adjectives up for sale

now diagram the sentence

from *The Nation*

JAMES RICHARDSON

Subject, Verb, Object

◇   ◇   ◇

I is not ego, not the sum
of your unique experiences,
just, democratically,
whoever's talking,
a kind of motel room,
yours till the end—
that is, of the sentence.

The language, actually,
doesn't think *I*'s important,
stressing, even in
grandiose utterances—
e.g., I *came*
I *saw* I *conquered*—
the other syllables.

Oh, it's a technical problem,
sure, the rhyme
on so-so-open
lie, cry, I
harder to stitch tight
than the ozone
hole in the sky.

But worst is its plodding insistence—
I, I, I—
somebody huffing uphill,
face red as a stop sign,

scared by a doctor
or some *He She It*
surprised in the mirror.

from *The New Yorker*

A Blind Astronomer in the Age of Stars

◊ ◊ ◊

He considers himself lucky to have been born
during the Age of Stars, all those beings
in their shimmering shades still flaring, their silent,
untouchable presence. He imagines how
they shine as if they were the work of light
giving sight, like eyes, to a blind universe.

Making his way through fields at night,
he can feel the light from those million
sources touching him like the particles
composing the finest airy fog, touching him
like the knowledge of lives in a silent forest.
He feels each star in the way he hears
each syllable of his lover's whisper.

And he claims to see the constellations
from the inside out, having been inscribed
from birth, he says, with their configurations.
Indeed his Braille depictions of Canis Major,
Dorado, Lyra, Orion, are to scale and perfect.
Often through summer nights, he lies on open
hillsides to observe the heavens. He describes
the stars as transforming his body with their patterns
like tattoos of light—the wings of Cygnus,
the horns of Taurus. What kind of fortune

would it be, he wonders, to feel the light
of the Southern Cross along his brow?

He believes that the constant *jeetz-a-jeetz*
of the wayside crickets and the notes of the reed
toads sounding like whistles underwater
and the soft-bristle brush of grasses in the wind,
all together match in cadence the multiple
spacings and motions of the stars. He imagines
that the sudden piercing cry of a rabbit or a prairie
mouse at night corresponds to the streak of a falling
meteor, a helpless descending diagonal of light.
He hears their passing in this way. The earth,
he is certain, is related to the starry sky by blood.

By the solid black existing behind his eyes,
he understands the dimension beyond the edge
of the farthest horizon, that place whose light
has not had time to reach and touch him. He knows
that place, its state and its lack. One he calls
Patience, the other *Pity.*

from *Alaska Quarterly Review*

John Clare's Finches

◇   ◇   ◇

I thought the first one was a leaf falling faster
Than any leaf could fall—no coasting the updrafts,
None of those sinuous floating undulations

That body forth the longing of anything falling
To return to the branch—and then it dipped and stalled
And touched its featherweight of gold to the fencepost,

And there we were, risen at dawn to breathe while we could
The vanishing cool of early late summer morning
And see the goldfinches should they chance to return—

And they came, but on a wind that never blew before:
I saw as in a rain-pool slicking the roadway
Or a shard of mirror lodged in a Romany's tree

The poor marvelous daft poet limping his way
Along the watery English lanes and by-lanes,
Humming the air of Highland Mary, dreaming his aim

Was taking him close and closer to remembered beauty—
Daisy, goldfinch, grass that smells of the baker's oven—
Who might have wrapped around him her arms long and small

Had she managed to breathe the air of his belief
And not die blameless and alone, sister to nothing
Or the bride of darkness, for all the difference it makes.

from *The New Republic*

JOHN RYBICKI

This Tape Measure Made of Light

◇　◇　◇

1.

We have some say in this skin we wear,
      the movie screen we paint over it.
We will it in public to be so and so,
      but there are red lights that halt
the steaming herd. We thank God for our hole,
      our hiding place, the hound
smacking its tail when we arrive, a kite
      ripping dumbly down our driveway.

2.

At a job site, snapped off from the familiar,
      we're lowering trusses onto a flat roof
then tying them together. There's a seven-
      story grain elevator spraying dust,
and what with the rain and the fermentation,
      we have a dairy farm on the roof,
a real shit storm to slop around in.
      We bang like this, our hammers
and our blood, to test along these verges,
      to hear something solid ringing back.
There's the hopper below us hissing
      and pouring nutritious pellets
for dogs and horses, pouring gravity—

fed into the big sacks. We climb
down the chute through this hole like a navel.
              Two men down there with earmuffs on,
and they're tossing the sacks onto a dolly all day.
              The young one senses animal
movement, my flicking a brush stroke
              of blood on him.
He looks up at me and nods
              and I nod back. It's an old light
that passes between us, and I make it
              into a nice rope, and I hold on.

3.

Take a pinch of light from under the rib:
              let's see how far it stretches:
this filament to measure your rafters
              to their tails, Lord.
How will you frame, say, a window
              in this house so a Milky Way
spills through it? Only so many fingers
              pinch at these fissures,
these light beams through
              every pore, every knothole.
What we long for or have lost
              lurks under those floorboards
we nail down knowing they're not floorboards.
              Our molecules rain outward,
which means we're always leaving
              someone. And our tired selves
line up behind us
              like men looking for work.

                    from *Third Coast*

Gravity and Grace

◊   ◊   ◊

Grace fills empty spaces, but it can only enter
where there is a void to receive it . . .
— Simone Weil

Simone Weil, it's hard to concentrate on you
with those three boys on the next bench
blowing up balloons and letting them go,
all squirt and grunt, fizzling into—

the void, I think you'd say. And leaving
a void too—if spent breath becomes exhaust,
if everything we do ends up empty.
So prayer, you'd add, becomes a little death

as we pour our desires into words
that fill to bursting, then leave our lips
to corkscrew and sputter into thin air,
selfless, anonymous enough to rise.

Now the boys race up the slide, all high-fives
and laughter, blowing off gravity, while I read
you'd like to be blown away, see a landscape
as it is when I am not there—as if the self

blocks God the way bodies block light.
Thus your executor was to destroy
all record of your mind—those notebooks filled
with stark meditations as Hitler railed,

as death camps filled and ghettos burned. *Love is
not consolation,* you wrote, *it is light,*
meaning that fierce headlamp of attention
which leaves the self in shadow and trains

its high beam on that void where prisoners
huddle under gravity's dark weight,
and grace, if it comes, comes in secret,
to those struck dumb, trembling in the glare.

from *Image*

Love

◊   ◊   ◊

with apologies to Julie Sheehan

I hate your kneecaps floating free
in their salty baths. I hate your knees,

both of them, and I hate your eyelashes,
especially the ones that fall out, the ones

you're supposed to wish on; I wish you
bad wishes. I hate every hair

on your hairy face, hate you as much
as I hate being put on hold,

thank you for your patience
when I have none, when patience

is as far away as my first grade teacher's
if you have nothing nice to say . . .

Your mushroom risotto: hate it.
The salmon you're defrosting: hate.

My vowels hate you.
My adverbs hate you. The backyard

hates you—the backyard with all its abandoned
dump trucks, with the giant hole our son dug

all summer while soaker hoses soaked. That hole
and all holes, including the hole in the ozone,

which of course keeps getting bigger.
Spaghetti wrapping around a fork.

Mashed spinach and carrots caught
in the rungs of a high chair, stuck

to the floor like dried green paint: hate,
hate, hate. Each furry rabbit a little furry ball

of hate. Each blackberry a messy drupe of drippy hate.
At the China Palace the plates piled high with Mu Shu

Hate, the plates now a busboy's burden of hate,
the only sound the dumpster's clanging *hate hate hate*.

from *The Cincinnati Review*

Like a Monkey

◇   ◇   ◇

Our sages tell us Rachel was a beautiful woman.
Light brown hair brown eyes
Five feet six or seven
Not a clothes horse
But always looked great whether getting ready for work
In white cashmere sweater pleated navy skirt
Or in the bleachers at a Cubs game
In cutoffs and t-shirt
Yet beside Sarah our sages tell us
Rachel was like a monkey
Rachel was like a monkey beside Sarah.
For our sages tell us Sarah was a beautiful woman
And most of all she loved to dance.
People try to move too much she said
Diamonds and rust on the stereo
Really you don't even need to move your feet.
You don't even need to move at all
Or just a little really
Yet beside Eve our sages tell us Sarah was like a monkey.
Sarah was like a monkey beside Eve.
For our sages tell us Eve was a beautiful woman
She dyed her hair to a metallic purple sheen
Wore matching purple eye shadow
And silver jewelry
Goth look but she made it work,
Teardrop tattoo by left eye
So small you might not even notice
And to the surprise of many she majored in cosmology
Physics journals on the floor

In her bathroom by the toilet
Yet beside Adam our sages tell us Eve was like a monkey
Eve was like a monkey beside Adam.
Beside Adam's foot our sages tell us
Eve was like a monkey
His foot shining brighter than the sun
Brighter than a thousand suns
Flash across the just-created sky
Fission burn
Of which though hidden,
A single spark still burns in you.

from *Jacket*

TOM SLEIGH

At the Pool

◊　◊　◊

The lifeguard, asleep,
                              slumps forward, at ease,
As if the Red Sea could be depended upon to part,
As if the waters themselves
                              would save the drowning.
My friend's wife has died
                              and as he tells how the thought

Of her having died,
                              being dead, her death and deadness
Being nothing he can stop now and that goes on and on,
He seems as he talks to be
                              his own Orpheus,
His own Eurydice
                              turning back on the stair each time

He calls her name,
                              turning around to climb
Back up, back down, the dead like a film
                              run backwards, forwards,
Forever approaching,
                              gliding away . . . My friend at 83
Still calling on his wife to come back to him,
                              making her

Climb up into the light—
                              the lifeguard's chiseled
Abdomen, rising,
                              falling, makes the pool water

Seem quieter, calmer in the shifting illuminations
And shadows wavering
                        of the underwater lights

That my friend,
                    who used to swim but can't now,
Once floated in front of
                        while we talked, taking
A break from doing laps,
                        his old man's
Muscles making his body seem somehow small

And huge, small in relation
                            to the pool bottom
Staring up through itself
                        like an oblivious, blank eye;
Huge in how his arms stretched out
                            made the whole pool's water
Seem to concentrate its buoyancy
                        just to float him.

from *AGNI*

VINCENT STANLEY

At the New York Public Library, I heard Derek Walcott dismiss the prose poem.

◊　◊　◊

(for Ryk Ekedal)

Disdained, the prose poem, by Walcott, his bluewater lilt curmudgeoned. Dismissed. No reason not to divide with a dot
I hear America calling for a dot
Sometimes a line strings possibilities too short to save—as
in an Agnes Martin drawing that fine rule won't quite reach the edge. And Freud
said the way back from fantasy to reality is art: well good luck, poem.

Feels a stranger to what's lyric poetry now, Walcott said, bluewater
lilt rising, and poetry is the language of grief he said.
Love lost, grief is—the poem sails on
afloat a dapple of pitch and roll, land rarely in line, so hard to tell
cargo from crates on a dock, what might groan timbers to
matchsticks and
sink us. Love comes to grief when so little by our effort is left to be won.

Americans for God's sake why don't you write about empire, Walcott growled.
Either for it or against! O but we can't see it that way.
As a Caribbean you feel the
soles of our feet but we feel the sand. Used to be
our business was business: steel, fine tolerances at speed—
Scott Fitzgerald driving drunk into the eye.

Now our America means this infinite
line, a bridge dot to dot: and each island bridged loses its bluewater name
and memory. Art couldn't carry us all the way back.
      Still the prose poem, however keenly
             off, its nose broken by masters,
snubs empire. Or misses the point. Or so I float as far as I got. True
too that lines in their shimmer (as a bridge over bentwood and hollow)
spell the deeps—those taut strings. How the lyric can lie yet the grief sound throug

from *Fulcrum*

Forty

◇   ◇   ◇

(for Daniel Pearl, in memoriam)

When did numbers hijack my life of words?
Until today words were everything; numbers nothing.
All changed at 40
when numbers exploded like nails from a suicide bomber.
1 life.
1 lunch hour, 5-mile run, 40 minutes;
10-minute shower; board meeting at 2.
200 dollars per month at 11 percent × 20 years = retirement.
Drop off child at 8; pick up child before 7.
600 thousand dollars of life insurance.
One life.
One dream of trees, tall sycamores perforated by light;
children as trees, inhaling, exhaling light,
and trees the only thing that matters.
One dream carrying my grandmother in my arms
and she weighs exactly the same as my child.
One beloved child.
123 trees in Independence Square Park.
100 thousand fragments of glass in the Parrish-Tiffany Mosaic;
260 colors.
One hawk perched on the weathervane—
rapacious, free.
One Colossus consecrated to the sun;
one Rome, thousands of Visigoths.
911
2 towers 101 stories 2 planes
3 thousand dead.

One evening in Florida the sun, hand over hand, drags notes
from doves' throats like strands of tears.
1 evening after the news, 5-mile run, 40 minutes,
24-hour deadline: one journalist: Pearl.
Palm fronds clatter and shift in the porous light:
clockwise; counter-clockwise.

from *American Poetry Review*

Heartlines

◊   ◊   ◊

Listen to your heart, this new man tells me. We are in a bar
with red velvet curtains for walls, sashes of conversation

draped under music. He pours rum and then Coke over ice,
which rattles like elegant gravel. When I listen to my heart,

I hear tires crunching on a dirt road years out of this city:
thrum-pulse of wood slats on the high-water bridge. I swam

after angel fish in that shallow creek, and though I'm sure
now they were trout, or less, I remember their fins' flirtatious

silver. Why is it that blood, which is most of our bodies,
disappears when we strike it with light? If I could, I'd spend

this night in my own heart, hear its off-metronome gurgle,
flowing and falling of darkness. I'd string bright lure, open

and fill the locks. In there, my father's fibrillated beat,
my mother's paling blood. In the red-lit elevator, he jokes

clever-drunkenly of Dante, though next day, riding down
nine floors in sheer silence, I do not think of hell,

but of a heart—awkwardly standing in a single chamber
as the cables lower us into our outside skins. I never see

this man again: a classical pianist stockbroker who promised
to seduce me with music. I remember these notes

like the seventy-five counties of a state I seldom visit, useless
even when I learned them as a child, unforgettably, by heart.

from *New England Review*

CRAIG MORGAN TEICHER

Ultimately
Justice Directs Them

◊   ◊   ◊

1

The soldiers are coming.
The soldiers
            are coming to break America.
The soldiers are dispatched
from America
            and they are landing
their boats on American shores.

2

Why are the soldiers coming?
Not because they believe
                        in what
they were told
            but because they believe
that ultimately justice directs them,
that ultimately
            the right thing will happen.

3

We say they are
the soldiers, but they are not:

they have eyes and
                    hands
and hairstyles and children
and expressions on their faces

that their mothers remember
on the faces
            of the infants they were.

4

They are coming to break
everything down
                to basics: America

has become too frumpy
for its pants.
                Its health
care system cares not
                    for health.

5

Its laws are more paper.

6

Its schools are more paper.

7

Its schools are brick and paper.

8

That is what the soldiers will say.

9

America looks at itself
and sees
itself, not America.

10

Itself looks at itself
and calls
what it sees America.

11

America has begun
calling everything
America no matter what.

12

Now more than ever.

13

Operation America.
Operation With Extra Cheese.

Operation With Fries With That.
Operation No Child Left Behind.

Operation Enduring Sandwich.
Operation Regurgitated Eagle.

Operation Prince of Freedom.
Operation All Night Long.

Operation Perhaps.
Operation No Really.

14

—

15

The soldiers are here.

16

Operation Big Time Pause.

17

Operation Please
                    And Thank You.

18

Operation Paper.
Operation No More Stars.

19

The Soldiers are wearing
yellow ribbons
                in support
of the return
                of the regular guy.

20

The soldiers are on TV
right outside
                the door.

21

They are knocking—change
the channel.

22

Operation America Go!
Operation Yes!

Operation OK, OK.
Operation Every Man
                for himself
and best of luck
                to the women and kids.

23

—

24

By part 24 it is
          already done.

from *No Tell Motel*

Liturgy

◊   ◊   ◊

—for the Mississippi Gulf Coast

To the security guard staring at the gulf
thinking of bodies washed away from the coast, plugging her ears
against the bells and sirens—sound of alarm—the gaming floor
on the coast;

To Billy Scarpetta, waiting tables on the coast, staring at the gulf
thinking of water rising, thinking of New Orleans, thinking of cleansing
the coast;

To the woman dreaming of returning to the coast, thinking of water rising,
her daughter's grave, my mother's grave—underwater—on the coast;

To Miss Mary, somewhere;

To the displaced, living in trailers along the coast, beside the highway,
in vacant lots and open fields; to everyone who stayed on the coast,
who came back—or cannot—to the coast;

To those who died on the coast.

This is a memory of the coast: to each his own
recollections, her reclamations, their
restorations, the return of the coast.

This is a time capsule for the coast: words of the people
—don't forget us—
the sound of wind, waves, the silence of graves,

the muffled voice of history, bulldozed and buried
under sand poured on the eroding coast,
the concrete slabs of rebuilding the coast.

This is a love letter to the Gulf Coast, a praise song, a dirge,
invocation and benediction, a requiem for the Gulf Coast.

This cannot rebuild the coast; it is an indictment, a complaint,
my *logos*—argument and discourse—with the coast.

This is my *nostos*—my pilgrimage to the coast, my memory, my reckoning—

native daughter: I am the Gulf Coast.

from *The Virginia Quarterly Review*

A Sea-Change

◇   ◇   ◇

With a change of government the permanent cobalt,
the promises we take with a pinch of salt,
with a change of government the permanent aquamarine,
with a reorganized cabinet the permanent violet,
the permanent lilac over the reef, the permanent flux
of ocher shallows, the torn bunting of the currents
and the receding banners of the breakers.
With a change in government no change in the cricket's chirrup,
the low, comical bellow of the bull, or
the astonishing symmetry of tossing horses.
With a change in government the haze of wide rain
which you begin to hear as the ruler hears the crowd
gathering under the balcony, the leader who has promised
the permanent cobalt of a change of government
with the lilac and violet of his cabinet change.

from *AGNI* and *Harper's*

Holding Action

Letters, be the memory of this moment,
Ruth's 3-legged Golden Lab
sniffing for news beneath the hedge,
grass glittering with rain,
the bird feeder mangled by our car.

Years from now I want to remember
how we walked the splendid earth
and saw it. When children read this
and smile at its old-fashioned vision,
then words, stubborn little boxcars

lugging meaning across the rickety
wood bridge to the future, hold,
hold. Couple against time, bear
the red geranium, the slender birch—
you, sentences—glitter against

the massive dark of nothing. Tell
of feet that buffed this doorsill
till it gleams, of cartwheeling
children. Remember the Rosetta
stone, the hum of Xerox machines,

remember monks copying, how
a prisoner in solitary picked up
a pebble to scribble stories
on the wall. Letters, I tell you,
even if your paper yellows in the attic,

even if it's torn and thrown into the sea,
each of you separate from your brothers,
swim through the ocean, row across
the sky, walk through the wasteland,
find a reader. Stay together. Hold.

from *The Hudson Review*

RONALD WALLACE

No Pegasus

◊   ◊   ◊

It looked a lot like a poem; it had lines
that preached enjambment; it had rhymes, of sorts,
both approximate and exact. It stopped on dimes.
Then started up again. It had cohorts—

metaphor and imagery and such—
and liked to keep time by beating on its
chest, though some might have said it walked with a crutch
and took more liberties than most of its fellow sonnets.

But it wasn't a poem, or at least it said it wasn't.
For who would want to be so small a thing?
It wanted to be a novel, and who doesn't?

It hid its horsy face, its tail, its wing,
under a cloak of prose. It stopped prancing.
But try as it might, it could not not sing.

from *Margie: The American Journal of Poetry*

Her Last Conflagration

◊　　◊　　◊

The moon's orange wind-tunnel ignites a smoldering
sky. Power poles loom like crosses many Jesuses
jumped down from, burning. My car flames in the murk:

red Firebird I've dumped my every cent into, then
wonder why the tires are flat. "Copper's heavy, man,"
my best friend gasps before flames pop him like the luna

moth that hit Dad's bug-zapper when I was 9, attempting
my first kiss. The heart-stopper who started this
has crackling orange hair. Heat-waves shimmer off

her skin. I look up from the raw armadillo I'm gnawing
for Survival Class, and watch her antelope across
a grove of live (for now) oak trees. Their acorns gleam

like carameled amethysts in steam. She makes me feel
tres troglodytic. "Priapism has its price," she'll say,
and pocket all my change. I've soaked in rainbow-

colored oils, and chewed my skin to soften it for her.
I've worn white wigs and wooden teeth since she said,
"General George can Yankee Doodle Do me any time."

She claims I make her feel like Mary in the *Pietà*,
cradling a wiener-dog in sunglasses and tie. "Just
like that, Pathos turns to Bathos, Lust to Bust," she cries,

a crazed look in her eyes—no, a napalm launcher
in her hand. She's always had it, but love blinded me.
Poof!—the veranda flares. And the Veronica (her name).

I just have time to clean the catbox, kiss her crispy
corpse and—fire carousing in the trees—say,
"Goodnight," with black lips, and some irony.

from *Salt Hill*

Leaving
Saint Peter's Basilica

◊　◊　◊

It isn't only the marble, the tombs of bronze,
the rigid brilliance of the angled stones,
the columns lined with purpose, glossed with time.

It's the shadow across the palm of someone's hand,
the action stopped: the folds of angels' robes
forever folded, the outstretched arms of popes

who supplicate or bless or mouth a prayer
with static, gesturing limbs. It's all the layers
hidden from us, the dust that's flesh entombed,

the sculptures of the women looking down
and one of two great lions, claws unsheathed
—vigilant, though their stone eyes look on nothing.

And last and least, it's me hunched on a pew,
scribbling to the light of burning candles,
trying to hide the sacrilege of writing

from all the other watchful bodies here,
those hardened into statue and those moving
steadily, until they trickle out

from the confines of the church. Sublime
extravagance, we find it, as we exit
into the portico and out the doors,

putting some space between it and ourselves
until the dome reappears, its arcs aglow,
the dusk-lit clouds around it pinkish white

and drifting past in gilded lumps like stucco
or bodies of other angels, selves, contorted,
rapturous, and—finally—dissolved.

from *Measure*

"This dream the world is having about itself . . ."

◊　◊　◊

—William Stafford

won't let us go. The western sky gathers
its thunderclouds. It has no urgent need

of us. That summer in our late teens we
walked all evening through town—let's say Cheyenne—

we were sisters at the prairie's edge: I
who dreamed between sage-green pages, and you

a girl who feared you'd die in your twenties.
Both of us barefoot, wearing light summer

dresses from the Thirties, our mother's good
old days, when she still believed she could live

anywhere, before her generation
won the War and moved on through the Forties.

As we walked, a riderless tricycle
rolled out slowly from a carport, fathers

watered lawns along the subdivisions'
treeless streets. We walked past the last houses

and out of the Fifties, the Oregon
Trail opened beneath our feet like the dream

of a furrow turned over by plough blades
and watered by Sacajawea's tears.

What did the fathers think by then, dropping
their hoses without protest as we girls

disappeared into the Sixties? We walked
all night, skirting the hurricane-force winds

in our frontier skirts so that the weather
forecasts for the Seventies could come true,

the Arapahoe's final treaties for
the inland ranges could fulfill themselves

ahead of the building sprees. We walked on
but where was our mother by then? Your lungs

were filling with summer storms, and my eyes
blurred before unrefracted glacial lakes.

Limousines started out from country inns
at the center of town, they meant to drive

our grandparents deep into their eighties.
Our mother in her remodeled kitchen

whispered our names into her cordless phone
but before the Nineties were over, both

of you were gone. Mother's breath was shadow
but her heart beat strong all the way in to

the cloud wall. You carried your final thoughts
almost to the millennium's edge, where

the westward-leaning sky might have told us
our vocation: in open fields, we would

watch the trail deepen in brilliant shadow
and dream all the decades ahead of us.

In memory of my sister

from *The Iowa Review*

Cinderella's Last Will & Testament

◊ ◊ ◊

No one ever mentions the executor's post-mortem
disposition of her one glass shoe,
its mate made a part of the property division
in the divorce proceedings years earlier.
The tiara. Satin gloves. Crystal-sequined clutch.
All souvenirs of the pivotal night that began everything.

The long-dead Disney mice fixed life-like
by her taxidermist brother-in-law. Small, dark marbles
instead of beads used to fill the gaps of their eye sockets,
reasonable facsimiles of their beady little eyes.
Each mouse re-dressed with kerchiefs
over the paper-thin cups of their ears,
muslin skirts and aprons wrapped around
their aged rodent waistlines, proof
of a lifetime of breakfasts and dinners
comprised of fatty nuts and corn.
In death, they are propped in positions
of relaxed repose against dioramas of meadows, mountains,
not washing a thimble basin
or stitching lace for princesses
or scurrying away alongside baseboards
as in life.

To the historical society, her diaries
detailing her riches to rags to riches story.

To the permanent collection
of the local textile museum, her gowns,
preserved in acid-free tissue.

Her tradition of philanthropy and charity balls
thrown for village gentry and peasants alike,
abandoned in her absence.

So far as we know, these things are gone.
Gone from the castle, gone from the grounds,
gone from the remnants of the progeny-less Charming estate.

But what of the mice?
Where have the mice gone?

from *OCHO*

I shall be released

◇   ◇   ◇

What we love
    will leave us

or is it
    we leave

what we love,
    I forget—

Today, belly
    full enough

to walk the block
    after all week

too cold
    outside to smile—

I think of you, warm
    in your underground room

reading the book
    of bone. It's hard going—

your body a dead
    language—

I've begun
    to feel, if not

hope then what
    comes just after—

or before—
    Let's not call it

regret, but
    this weight,

or weightlessness,
    or just

plain waiting.
    The ice wanting

again water.
    The streams of two planes

a cross fading.

I was so busy
    telling you this I forgot

to mention the sky—
    how in the dusk

its steely edges
    have just begun to rust.

from *The Kenyon Review*

Never to Return

◊   ◊   ◊

Today a ladybug flew through my window. I was reading
about the snowy plumage of the willow ptarmigan
and the song of the Nashville warbler. I was reading
the history of weather, how they agreed at last
to disagree on cloud categories. I was reading a chronicle
of the boredom that called itself The Great Loneliness
and caused a war. I was reading mosquitoes rode
to Hawaii on the same ship that brought the eucalyptus
to California to function now as a terrible fire accelerator.
Next to me almost aloud a book said doctors can
already transplant faces. Another said you know January
can never be June so why don't you sleep little candle?
A third one murmured some days are too good,
they had to have been invented in a lab. I was paging
through a book of unsent postcards. Some blazed
with light, others were a little dim as if someone
had breathed on the lens. In one it forever snowed
on a city known as the Emerald in Embers, the sun had
always just gone behind the mountains, never to return,
and glass buildings over the harbor stayed filled with
a sad green unrelated light. The postcard was called
The Window Washers. In handwriting it said
Someone left an important window open, and Night
the black wasp flew in and lay on the sill and died.
Sometimes I stop reading and find long black hairs
on my keyboard and would like you to know that in 1992
I mixed Clairol dye no. 2 with my damaged bleached hair
to create a blue-green never seen before, my best look

according to the girl at the counter who smiled only once,
I know less than I did before, and I live on a hill where
the wind steals music from everything and brings it to me.

from *The Paris Review*

CONTRIBUTORS' NOTES AND COMMENTS

JOHN ASHBERY was born in Rochester, New York, in 1927. His *Notes from the Air: Selected Later Poems* (Ecco, 2007) won the 2008 Griffin International Prize for Poetry. *The Landscapist,* his collected translations of the poetry of Pierre Martory, was published in 2008 by Sheep Meadow Press in the United States and Carcanet in the United Kingdom. The Library of America published the first volume of his *Collected Poems* in fall 2008. He was the guest editor of *The Best American Poetry 1988,* the inaugural volume in this series.

Of "They Knew What They Wanted," Ashbery writes: "This poem is a collage of movie titles. I came upon it, almost fully formed, while consulting one of Leonard Maltin's film guides one day. Suddenly a poem seemed to jump out at me. In a way it's kind of a sequel to a poem called 'He' that I wrote in 1953, in which every line began with the pronoun 'he.' I can't guarantee that there won't be a sequel since there are a few personal pronouns left."

CALEB BARBER was born in Bellingham, Washington, in 1983. He still lives there, working days in an aerospace machine shop. He has a BA from Western Washington University and an MFA from the Northwest Institute of Literary Arts based off Whidbey Island. In the near future, his book of poems, *Beasts and Violins,* will be published by Red Hen Press.

Barber writes: "I wrote the poem 'Beasts and Violins' while driving on the interstate, coming back from work. I was listening to country music—good country music, a band called the Handsome Family. Their songs got me thinking about the appreciation of lonesomeness, so I started writing the piece on a notepad on my knee, pretending my life could have been a little bit like Hank Williams's at certain points. It's a personal poem, for sure, but I wanted the ending to leave all that behind, so I took it to a place I've never been: a train either in Russia or Canada, probably thirty years or more before I was born."

MARK BIBBINS was born in Albany, New York, in 1968. He lives in New York City and teaches at the New School and Columbia University. His books of poems are *The Dance of No Hard Feelings* (Copper Canyon Press, 2009) and the Lambda Award–winning *Sky Lounge*. Recent work has appeared in the *Paris Review, New England Review, Barrow Street,* the anthology *Satellite Convulsions* (Tin House Books, 2008), and the online project *Starting Today: Poems for the First 100 Days*. In 2005 he was a New York Foundation for the Arts fellow.

Of "Concerning the Land to the South of Our Neighbors to the North," Bibbins writes: "The last line kicked it off, on a train rattling along the Connecticut coastline, but it felt like it was going somewhere else (the train, not the poem, which was circuitous but inevitable). Joe Lieberman was about to lose the Senate primary to Ned Lamont.

"The facts are invented, though not all of them by me. The Alaskan entry came long before a certain former mayor got too much attention—prophecy isn't all it's cracked up to be—and I hope never to encounter leather pie. Also, I realized after writing the poem that it's a sort of gawky distant cousin of John Ashbery's 'Into the Dusk-Charged Air,' to which the former tips its star-spattered hat."

BRUCE BOND was born in Pasadena, California, in 1954. He has written seven collections of poetry, including *Blind Rain* (Louisiana State University Press, 2008), *Cinder* (Etruscan Press, 2003), *The Throats of Narcissus* (University of Arkansas, 2001), *Radiography* (TIL Best Book of Poetry Award, BOA Editions, 1997), *The Anteroom of Paradise* (Colladay Award, QRL, 1991), *Independence Days* (R. Gross Award, Woodley Press, 1990), and a forthcoming volume entitled *Peal* (Etruscan Press, 2010). He has received fellowships from the National Endowment for the Arts and the Texas Commission on the Arts. He is Regents Professor of English at the University of North Texas and poetry coeditor of *American Literary Review*.

Of "Ringtone," Bond writes: "As with any tragedy, the Virginia Tech shooting had the effect of bringing strangers together in their grief, including worried parents and the unfamiliar voices who answered the phones of the dead. I had a hard time wrapping my head around how difficult this would be for the parents, obviously, but also for the medics who carted away the bodies, who found themselves in the awkward situation of speaking with such simultaneous intimacy and distance. The situation focuses what it is when tragedy lays a sudden claim on you, when you are called upon, with little warning, to respond with a kind of grace, not unlike the poise of an art that wears its art lightly, that calls upon the genuine and clear to break the unspeakable news."

MARIANNE BORUCH was born in Chicago, Illinois, in 1950. A graduate of the University of Illinois, Urbana, and the University of Massachusetts, Amherst, she has taught at Tunghai University in Taiwan, at the University of Maine at Farmington, and, since 1987, at Purdue University and in the low-residency MFA program at Warren Wilson College. Her six collections of poetry include *Poems: New and Selected* (Oberlin, 2004) and most recently *Grace, Fallen from* (Wesleyan, 2008). Her two books of essays about poetry are in print: *Poetry's Old Air* (Michigan, 1993) and *In the Blue Pharmacy* (Trinity, 2005). *Ghost & Oar,* a chapbook of poems she wrote as an artist-in-residence at Isle Royale National Park, was published by Red Dragonfly Press in 2007. She has received fellowships from the National Endowment for the Arts and the Guggenheim Foundation. She lives in West Lafayette, Indiana, with her husband.

Boruch writes: "'The Doctor' is a poem about getting older, I suppose, the mind forced to think directly about the body and its shy, unruly citizenry of joints and vessels, blood and bone, eye and heart and lung previously invisible when all ran right. This has to be a backhanded gift of living past fifty, the need to attend to such things. Thus the world widens even as it threatens to close or at least tilt sideways in that semi-dark. One can be amused or not, amazed or not. My own doctor, Amanda Curnock, is a marvel of curiosity and sense. Which is why this poem is dedicated to her."

FLEDA BROWN was born in Columbia, Missouri, in 1944. She is professor emerita at the University of Delaware, was Delaware poet laureate for six years beginning in 2001, and now lives in Traverse City, Michigan. She teaches in the Rainier Writing Workshop low-residency MFA program in Tacoma, Washington. She won the Felix Pollak Prize for her collection of poems, *Reunion* (University of Wisconsin Press, 2007). Five previous collections have appeared: *The Women Who Loved Elvis All Their Lives* (Carnegie Mellon University Press, 2004), *Breathing In, Breathing Out* (Anhinga Press, 2002), *The Devil's Child* (Carnegie Mellon, 1999), *Do Not Peel the Birches* (Purdue, 1993), and *Fishing with Blood* (Purdue University Press, 1988). She has a collection of essays, *Driving with Dvořák,* forthcoming from the University of Nebraska Press in spring 2010.

Of "Roofers," Brown writes: "The roofers are pounding overhead on the cottage, and I start hearing the church-camp song, 'Over my head, there's music in the air / there must be a God somewhere.' I don't know whether the poem begins with that in my head, or with the sound of the goofy roofers slapping down shingles, that makes me think of the huge feet of clowns, then of Shakespeare's clowns, then of those other lowly ones whose work makes possible the work of the mightier gods. And who else makes the work of the gods possible? Milton, Hopkins, the gods of God-literature.

"In my notebook, I find, 'There had to be a god somewhere because of the singing, drawn forth by it, lifted by it above our heads because of the voices, the throat tightening to make the sounds (here, apparently, is where the thought of smallness begins to enter the poem), the constriction necessary for music, a roof like a meter (I may have been thinking of the regularity of shingles, and of the constriction a roof makes, a holding in), like a turning back upon itself, constantly referring to itself, or referring the contents back upon itself. At church camp, 'Tell Me Why, etc., all referring as we knew back to God, it would all turn back to that, the heat and the breeze and the spillway rocks, all of this a calculation of the roof, holding us as if we were in a shadow box . . .'

"That's where the shadow box enters the poem. I used to love those things. I made them out of shoe boxes, taping little cardboard people and trees upright inside. I don't know if what I describe is the sequence of my mind. All I can do, really, is explicate my own poem. The word that made the poem settle into place for me, when I finally found it, was 'tenderness.' It turns the speaker back to the child she was, giving her that word like a roof over that child's head."

Born on the eastern shore of Maryland (1967) and raised there by wolves and vultures, CATHERINE CARTER now lives in Cullowhee with her husband near Western Carolina University, where she teaches in and coordinates the English education program. Her first book, *The Memory of Gills* (LSU, 2006), received the 2007 Roanoke-Chowan Award from the North Carolina Literary and Historical Association.

Carter writes: "'The Book of Steve' (or 'Adam and Steve') was written in 2005; I was an adult before I heard the epigram 'God made Adam and Eve, not Adam and Steve,' which is commonly used as a justification for homophobia. It struck me as a strange rationale: it implies that if only Genesis had said that God *did* make Adam and Steve, there never would have been any homophobia, and if the book I imagined turned up and were authenticated, the speakers would immediately embrace their gay, lesbian, bisexual, or transgendered fellows with open arms. I probably don't have to add that I don't think that's true. But the idea appealed to me; why shouldn't there be a Book of Steve? There are creation texts out there that treat animals as significant and don't espouse dominion over the earth; I don't know of any right now that also imply commentary about keeping population size reasonable, or don't focus on heterosexuals, but that doesn't mean they weren't written.

"This paragraph makes the poem sound very didactic, and maybe it came out that way; but while all that was certainly underneath, it wasn't the sole intent. Poems grow around specifics, so I love the picture of Steve forever in Eden, unchronicled; of the apples being unicorn fodder; of there being some comic side, in the sense of happy endings, to all this struggle and stress about what the holy books say and what values they do, or don't, justify. For me, this is a fairly lighthearted poem, and I hope it gives pleasure and amusement, solace as well as sentence."

SUZANNE CLEARY was born in Binghamton, New York, in 1955. Her poetry books are *Trick Pear* (2007) and *Keeping Time* (2002), both published by Carnegie Mellon University Press. She has won the Cecil Hemley Memorial Award of the Poetry Society of America. She is professor of English at SUNY Rockland and reviews books for *Bloomsbury Review*.

Of "From *The Boy's Own Book: A Compleat Encyclopedia of All the Diversions Athletic, Scientific, and Recreative, of Boyhood and Youth*, by William Clarke," Cleary writes: "I might write more poems if I spent less time at flea markets, but I am irresistibly drawn to the worn, the cast off, the forgotten, the old, the handmade, the lead-painted mass-produced. Especially ephemera, and fabrics.

"I loved the feel in my hand of William Clarke's thick little book with the long name, and so, dear reader, I married him to some ideas about mortality and mystery. The nameless boy featured throughout the book seems to stand for anyone who has ever wondered how best to pass the unknowable number of days we are each given."

BILLY COLLINS was born in the French Hospital in New York City in 1941. He was an undergraduate at Holy Cross College and received his PhD from the University of California, Riverside. His books of poetry include *Ballistics* (Random House, 2008), *The Trouble with Poetry and Other Poems* (Random House, 2005), a collection of haiku titled *She Was Just Seventeen* (Modern Haiku Press, 2006), *Nine Horses* (Random

House, 2002), *Sailing Alone Around the Room: New and Selected Poems* (Random House, 2001), *Picnic, Lightning* (University of Pittsburgh Press, 1998), *The Art of Drowning* (University of Pittsburgh Press, 1995), and *Questions About Angels* (William Morrow, 1991), which was selected for the National Poetry Series by Edward Hirsch and reprinted by the University of Pittsburgh Press in 1999. He is the editor of *Poetry 180: A Turning Back to Poetry* (Random House, 2003) and *180 More: Extraordinary Poems for Every Day* (Random House, 2005). He is a distinguished professor of English at Lehman College (City University of New York). A frequent contributor and former guest editor of *The Best American Poetry* series, he was appointed United States Poet Laureate 2001–2003 and served as New York State Poet 2004–2006.

Of "The Great American Poem," Collins writes: "Proclaiming the superiority of poetry to prose, especially fiction, is a bad habit of mine, and here I have indulged in it again. Is it just my sour-grapes reaction to the mesmerizing popularity of fiction, the kind that can turn a novel into a 'major motion picture'? Would I be standing on firmer ground if I cited the antiquity of poetry—its decisively premodern origins? Its durability? Its concision? Its freedom from the bonds of social realism? Its fastidious occupation of the page? I once tried to conclude a debate on the subject by pointing out that poetry was a bird and prose a potato—a solid closer, I thought, but the discussion dragged on. Sure, the argument may be endless and even pointless, but in 'The Great American Poem,' I am trying again to have the last word. To that end, the intimacy and mysteriousness of poetry is privileged over the novel's usually unavoidable vulgarity (sex/violence) as well as the blatant stimulation of plot (gee, what next?).

"The closing image of a field of crickets as the sound of meditative silence is one I once heard from the hipster-guru Robert Hall on a visit to his lair in Todos Santos, Mexico."

ROB COOK was born in Phillipsburg, New Jersey, in 1969. He is the author of three collections of poems: *Songs for the Extinction of Winter* (Rain Mountain Press, 2006), *Diary of Tadpole the Dirtbag* (Rain Mountain Press, 2009), and *Blackout Country* (BlazeVOX, 2009). He lives in Manhattan's East Village with his girlfriend and two cats and works (very) sporadically as a freelance editor.

Cook writes: "'The Song of America' was written during a very frightening nine-day period of heart arrhythmia, due probably to a change in my psychotropic medication, thanks to my incompetent psychiatrist. I was also listening to a lot of Gary Moore, David Gilmour, Solas, Leonard Cohen, Tears For Fears, Joan Armatrading, and Ronnie Montrose."

JAMES CUMMINS was born in Columbus, Ohio, in 1948, and grew up in the Midwest, primarily in Cleveland and Indianapolis. He received a BA from the University of Cincinnati and an MFA from the University of Iowa Writers' Workshop. His first book, *The Whole Truth,* was published by North Point Press in 1986, and his second, *Portrait in a Spoon,* by the University of South Carolina Press in 1997. *The Whole Truth* was reissued in the Carnegie Mellon University Press "Classic Contemporary Series" in 2003. His third book, *Then & Now,* was published by Swallow Press (Ohio University Press) in 2004. A fourth book, *Jim & Dave Defeat the Masked Man,* written collaboratively with David Lehman and collecting the sestinas written to date by the two poets, was published by Soft Skull Press in 2006. Cummins has been curator of the Elliston Poetry Collection at the University of Cincinnati since 1975, where he is also a professor of English. He lives in Cincinnati with his wife, Maureen Bloomfield, a poet and art critic, and their two daughters, Katherine and Margaret.

Of "Freud," Cummins writes: "This poem is atypical for me and hard to write about. It comes out of many things: Bush-era frustration; Frederick Crews's vendetta against Freud; an identification with high modernist concerns that two thousand years of Western culture is 'in error'; a real loathing for so-called 'Christians'; my own father's death and my mother's debility, members of the 'greatest generation' destroyed by a depression and a world war and thus turned into perhaps the worst parenting generation in the history of the country; and a general dismay at the soullessness of a country that believes only in ones and zeroes. More than anything, it comes from a sense that our languages don't cohere. Two brief recent examples: Tom Daschle's $128,000 tax debt seems like a small fortune to someone like me, yet is just chump change to the 'players' at the top of our pyramid: sports figures, entertainers, politicians. Much as we working stiffs resent it, should it be a big enough deal to knock him out of the game if he is, in fact, the best qualified person to shepherd health reform through the intricacies of 'the Hill'? And the second: Rick, the man my age who's been fixing our plumbing for twenty years, came over the week after the inauguration. I asked him what he thought about it. He said, 'I don't know, Jim; I hate socialism.' Our languages just don't have the same meanings at different class and economic levels of our society. Maybe the writer's charge now is no longer to make it new, but to make it cohere."

MARK DOTY was born in Maryville, Tennessee, in 1953. After ten years of teaching at the University of Houston, he recently joined the faculty at Rutgers University in New Brunswick, New Jersey. He lives in New York City and on the east end of Long Island. The most recent of his eight books of poems is *Fire to Fire: New and Selected Poems* (HarperCollins, 2008), which won the National Book Award for Poetry. He has also published four volumes of nonfiction prose, the newest of which is *Dog Years* (HarperCollins, 2007), which won the Israel Fishman Non-fiction Award from the American Library Association.

Of "Apparition (Favorite Poem)," Doty writes: "I was in a dim mood about the future of poetry when I went to one of the Favorite Poem Project readings at a bookstore in Houston. When a high school student there recited Shelley's 'Ozymandias,' I felt heartened by the old sonnet's persistence and power—and the experience felt richer and more complicated because it happened to be a poem about the folly of power, about the way that nothing persists. Later I read my poem at that same bookstore, and who should be in the audience but that same young man and his parents; they'd read my poem on their own, and felt pleased by it. There was something happily communal about reading the poem to them, in the same space where it began, as if the poem and its afterlife were part of an exchange of gifts—from Shelley to the young man, from him to me, from me to him and his family, so that we strangers were brought together through the odd way that poetry connects us, across time and distance."

DENISE DUHAMEL was born in Providence, Rhode Island, in 1961. Her most recent books are *Ka-Ching!* (University of Pittsburgh Press, 2009), *Two and Two* (Pittsburgh, 2005), *Mille et un Sentiments* (Firewheel, 2005), *Queen for a Day: Selected and New Poems* (Pittsburgh, 2001), *The Star-Spangled Banner* (Southern Illinois University Press, 1999), and *Kinky* (Orchises Press, 1997). A bilingual edition of her poems, *Afortunada de mí* (Lucky Me), translated into Spanish by Dagmar Buchholz and David Gonzalez, came out in 2008 with Bartleby Editores (Madrid). She is an associate professor of English at Florida International University in Miami.

Duhamel writes: "'How It Will End' was written following a walk on the beach very much like the one described in this poem. I was interested in the way the speaker and her husband were able to observe and judge another couple in crisis—poor things!—rather than look at their own relationship. Or alternately, looking at the young couple gave the speaker and her husband a way to talk about their failing relationship. This is a poem of witness and of admission."

ALICE FRIMAN was born in New York City in 1933. Her ninth collection of poetry is *Vinculum,* forthcoming from Louisiana State University Press. Other recent books are *The Book of the Rotten Daughter* (2006) and *Inverted Fire* (1997), both from BkMk Press, and *Zoo* (University of Arkansas Press, 1999), which won the Ezra Pound Poetry Award from Truman State University and the Sheila Margaret Motton Prize from the New England Poetry Club. She is also the author of four chapbooks. She has received fellowships from the Indiana Arts Commission, the Arts Council of Indianapolis, and the Bernheim Foundation; and she won the 2002 James Boatwright Prize from *Shenandoah.* She was a professor of English at the University of Indianapolis from 1973 to 1993 and now lives in Milledgeville, Georgia, where she is poet-in-residence at Georgia College & State University.

Friman writes: "'Getting Serious' was written while I was enjoying a month-long residency in the home of Carson McCullers in Columbus, Georgia. I was working on some very sober pieces about our summer trip to Peru: poems about the slaughter of eleven million Indians, the Spanish Inquisition, Saint James—otherwise known as Santiago, killer of Moors, later to be dubbed Santiago, Indian killer—not to mention poems about how I had struggled to breathe at sixteen thousand feet. Maybe it was all that serious stuff I was reading about religion and hypocrisy that put me in such an irreverent mood, but the first words of 'Getting Serious' just popped into my head, and from there on, following the thread was irresistible and irreversible."

MARGARET GIBSON was born in Philadelphia in 1944. She is the author of nine books of poems, most recently *One Body,* which won the Connecticut Book Award for Poetry in 2008, and the forthcoming *Second Nature.* Other titles, all from Louisiana State University Press, include *Long Walks in the Afternoon,* the Lamont Selection in 1982; *Memories of the Future; The Daybooks of Tina Modotti; The Vigil; Earth Elegy; New and Selected Poems* (1997); *Icon and Evidence* (2001); and *Autumn Grasses* (2003). A memoir, *The Prodigal Daughter,* was published by University of Missouri Press in 2008. Gibson has been awarded a National Endowment for the Arts Grant, grants from the Connecticut Commission on the Arts, and a Lila Wallace Reader's Digest Fellowship. She is professor emerita, University of Connecticut. She lives in Preston, Connecticut.

Of "Black Snake," Gibson writes: "I live within a hundred-acre land trust of woods, wetlands, ridges, brooks, and ponds—my closest neighbors are deer and bobcat, owl and hawk, midge and mosquito. Some of the creatures call my house their sometimes shelter, one in particular: a large black snake I've been privileged to observe for some years. While it is 'traditional' to regard animals, reptiles, and birds as separate from that which is human, I have been more intrigued by our interdependent and reciprocal presences and by the sensuous 'language' of the natural world. I regard the black snake as an experiencing subject, sensitive and responsive, and I 'listen' to it with respect. Readers should regard the final nine lines of the poem as a translation of what the speaker intuits the snake to be 'saying,' speaking from the depth of its nature to hers. The fire of Kundalini has been likened to serpent fire, and yes: my heart does pound when I sight the black snake that chooses my attic for a molting place, my mantel for a route, where to exactly I don't yet know."

DOUGLAS GOETSCH was born in Brooklyn, New York, in 1963. He is the author of three full-length books—*Nobody's Hell* (Hanging Loose Press, 1999), *The Job of Being Everybody* (Cleveland State, 2004), and *Nameless Boy* (unpublished)—and four chapbooks. He has received poetry fellowships from the National Endowment for the Arts and the New York Foundation for the Arts, and is a recent recipient of the Donald Murray Prize for creative nonfiction. For twenty-one years he taught high school in New York City. Currently he teaches in writing programs and conferences around the country, and is editor of Jane Street Press.

Of "First Time Reading Freud," Goetsch writes: "This poem came to me while waiting for the elevator on the second floor of Stuyvesant High School, where I taught. I smelled the odor mentioned in the beginning, but didn't know the source; I knew it harkened to something in the past, but didn't know that source either. Waiting for that elevator, in a packed school hallway teeming with life, often provided just enough respite in the day for me to sense how many great subjects were flying past my nose, never to be written about, during the years I spent as an overworked New York City high school English teacher.

But this one, for some reason, I wasn't letting go of. The situation by the elevator is never mentioned in the poem, but it may have something to do with its searching quality, its sense of struggling against a current of distraction for some meaning."

ALBERT GOLDBARTH was born in Chicago, Illinois, in 1948. He is Distinguished Professor of Humanities in the Department of English at Wichita State University. He has been publishing volumes of poetry (from trade publishers, university publishers, and independent literary presses) for thirty-five years; two of these have received the National Book Critics Circle Award. *The Kitchen Sink: New and Selected Poems 1972–2007* (Graywolf Press, 2008) was nominated for the *Los Angeles Times* Book Award and received the Binghamton University Milt Kessler Award. His latest collection is *To Be Read in 500 Years* (Graywolf, 2009).

"I don't believe in backgrounding the poem with extraneous material. The poem is here to speak on its own behalf, and I hope some people like it."

BARBARA GOLDBERG was born in Wilmington, Delaware, in 1943. She is the author of four books of poetry, most recently *The Royal Baker's Daughter,* recipient of the 2008 Felix Pollak Poetry Prize. Her other prize-winning books include *Berta Broadfoot and Pepin the Short, Cautionary Tales,* and *Marvelous Pursuits.* She has also coedited—and translated poems in—two anthologies of contemporary Israeli poetry, including *After the First Rain: Israeli Poems on War and Peace.* She has received two fellowships in poetry from the National Endowment for the Arts. She is senior speechwriter at AARP and teaches speechwriting, poetry, and translation at Georgetown University and at the Writer's Center in Bethesda, Maryland.

Of "The Fullness Thereof," Goldberg writes: "A composer friend of mine asked me for lyrics for *Singing the Blue Ridge,* a portion of a piece commissioned by a Virginia performing arts organization. And so I wrote 'The Fullness Thereof,' basing some of the text on eighteenth-century cartographer diaries. I wanted to get a feel for both the landscape and the language of the time. She couldn't use this particular poem, so I stashed it away. A few years later I rediscovered it and thought it wasn't half bad, and quite unlike anything I'd ever written. I love the title—a phrase from the opening of Psalm 24—and also combining three distinct dictions and time periods into a single poem."

MICHAEL J. GRABELL was born in 1981 and raised in Montville, New Jersey. He is an investigative reporter for ProPublica.org, a new journalism organization that has produced pieces for *60 Minutes,* the *New York Times,* and *USA Today.* He studied creative writing at Princeton University and is a mentor in the MFA program at Western Connecticut State University. Last summer, he moved from Dallas to Brooklyn, where he lives with his wife, Laura, and their beloved potted plants. He is working on his first book of poems.

Of "Definition of Terms," Grabell writes: "In the first creative writing class I ever taught, I was explaining an assignment in which the students would use an anecdote from their lives as the basis for a short story or poem. As I used the example of how my parents met, explaining all the symbolism one could extract from their having been fixed up by the kosher butcher in Weehawken, it occurred to me that I needed to write this poem. So I carved out some writing time and went over to my neighborhood Starbucks. The poem seemed to flow organically from the opening line as I traced out other family stories and images from growing up second-generation American in suburban New Jersey. I'm not sure exactly where the rhythm and structure came from. Maybe it was because I was reading a lot of legal documents as a court reporter for the *Dallas Morning News,* or maybe it was the singsong cadence of the barista as she announced, 'Venti triple nonfat macchiato!' Special thanks to the Writer's Garret in Dallas and the poets Jack Myers and Farid Matuk, who provided invaluable feedback as I revised this poem."

DEBORA GREGER was born in Walsenburg, Colorado, in 1949. She has published seven books of poetry, including *God* (2001) and *Western Art* (2004), both from Penguin USA. She teaches in the creative writing program at the University of Florida in Gainesville. Her work has appeared in several volumes of *The Best American Poetry,* most recently the 2006 anthology edited by Billy Collins.

JENNIFER GROTZ was born in Canyon, Texas, in 1971. She teaches at the University of Rochester and in the MFA program at Warren Wilson College and is the assistant director of the Bread Loaf Writers Conference. Her first book, *Cusp,* was published by Houghton Mifflin in 2003. Her poems, reviews, and translations from the French and Polish appear widely.

Grotz writes: "'The Record' is an amalgam of remembered images and sensations from one rainy winter in Portland, Oregon, when I worked as an editor by day and my beloved worked overnight shifts at the post office during the holiday rush. Images of the city, remembrance of blues songs, and our mutual love of Plato are embedded here. I wrote the poem years after the fact, alone in a different city, in a single sitting, in a kind of bewildered state of gratitude and grief. It felt more like I was singing the poem than writing it."

BARBARA HAMBY was born New Orleans, Louisiana, in 1952, and was raised in Honolulu, Hawaii, where her eighty-five-year-old mother still lives in tropical splendor. Since 1981 she has been married to sublime poet and molto fun guy David Kirby. They live and cook in Tallahassee, Florida, and teach at Florida State University, which has a fantastic study abroad program that allows them to live in exotic places on a regular basis. They have not sold their souls, as is commonly reported. Her first book, *Delirium* (North Texas, 1994), won the Vassar Miller Prize, the Kate Tufts Award, and the Poetry Society of America's Norma Farber First Book Prize. Her other books are *The Alphabet of Desire* (NYU Press, 1999) and *Babel* (Pittsburgh, 2004), winner of the AWP Donald Hall Prize. "Ode to Airheads, Hairdos, Trains to and from Paris" is in *All-Night Lingo Tango* (Pittsburgh, 2009).

Hamby writes: "'Ode to Airheads' was written in the fall of 2006 when David and I were living in Paris. Our apartment was near the Luxembourg gardens, and most days we took a walk there. It is a lovely place, but at the entrance we used, there is a plaque commemorating a Resistance fighter who was shot on that very spot by the Nazis. Here we were in this most civilized of cities—eating exquisite tarts and drinking wines far better than we deserved—and there were these constant reminders of the chaos that is always lurking.

"This poem is part of a third sequence of odes I have written. I first came to the ode through the Romantics, especially Keats, and Pablo Neruda. I loved the music of Keats's line and Neruda's elevation of ordinary things. However, after I finished my first sequence ('Ode to the Lost Luggage Warehouse at the Rome Airport' was in *The Best American Poetry 2000*), I began to read Pindar and Horace and really study the form. I loved Pindar's wild leaps and associations, and I was deeply moved by Horace's humor and intimacy. I found myself wanting to write a more formal poem, but, of course, there was no way I could translate the Greek and Latin forms into English nor did I want to. I wanted to write an ode that had structure but sounded entirely contemporary.

"I am metrically challenged. At a concert I have to look at other people to clap on the beat. However, I love to count, so I came up with a thirteen-syllable line (more or less). Inspired by Joseph Brodsky's 'Twenty Sonnets to Mary Queen of Scots,' I had a lot of fun with end rhymes. 'Ode to Airheads' owes more to Horace than Pindar. Pindaric odes jump around and are more public utterances, whereas Horatian odes seem to me to start off with a lot of surface dazzle, but they end looking at the dark loneliness that we try to push to the edges.

"I loved using this form. It really helped me make associations I wouldn't have if left to my own lazy devices. When I read these poems aloud, I hope they sound like free verse or at least a contemporary person talking and making associations, lost in her own mental movie."

SARAH HANNAH was born in Newton, Massachusetts, in 1966. She received a BA from Wesleyan University, and an MFA and a PhD with distinction from Columbia University. Her two books are *Longing Distance* (2004) and *Inflorescence* (2007), both from Tupelo Press. She was an editor at Barrow Street Press, and poet laureate of the Friends of Hemlock Gorge, an organization of nature conservators in Newton, Massachusetts. She was awarded a Governor's Fellowship for residencies at the Virginia Center for the Creative Arts for the summers of 2001, 2002, and 2006. Until her death in May 2007, she taught poetry writing and literature at Emerson College.

Jennifer Michael Hecht, a friend of Sarah Hannah, writes: "'The Safe House' had me convinced that it was a description of a film—one that I had seen. I went so far as to believe it starred Richard Widmark. A woman was at the center of the film, plotting as in *Double Indemnity* or *Body Heat;* she has a history of going nuts and burning things down, and she had tried to get a guy to do this heist scheme before but the chump had always been scared (of her) and died or got out of there. This guy, though, Widmark, is a little crazy, too, and is hot for how crazy she is.

"They plan that he'll take her secret information and her scheme. If he ever feels the moment is right, he'll do it. She better disappear before people find out the money is gone, so if it happens, she'll get a king of diamonds under her door, and a black Packard will come for her.

"For most of the film, she lives her normal life, but sometimes at night we see her driving past the hill, behind which there is an actual house, a cape, but inside more like a dormer, with a hot plate and a full bar. I get it that Sarah would still bother with the corset and its twelve little sonnet lines, I get the choice of no kitchen but a stocked bar. I see each scene as filmic memory: the card appears, the car appears; as she walks from the car to the safe house, her heels sink in the mud and she totters as if drunk. Once inside she is steady. I see her dress in gold, have a scotch, and wait. Then Widmark comes in and he looks messed up and hot, and he says he is her ace in the hole, and clamps his hands to her waist, and they kiss and they screw.

"I remember thinking, 'Oh, this is strange, this is working out, they are going to get away with it.' Then we see a gun, and then we see it is in her hands, and she is curling her finger around the trigger, and then the film is over."

JERRY HARP was born in 1961 and grew up in Mt. Vernon, Indiana. He has degrees from St. Meinrad College (BA), St. Louis University (MA), the University of Florida (MFA), and the University of Iowa (PhD). His books of poems are *Creature* (Salt, 2003), *Gatherings* (Ashland Poetry Press, 2004), and *Urban Flowers, Concrete Plains* (Salt, 2006). He coedited *A Poetry Criticism Reader* (University of Iowa Press, 2006). His forthcoming scholarly books are *"Constant Motion": Ongian Hermeneutics and the Shifting Ground of Early Modern Understanding* (Hampton Press) and *"For Us, What Music?": On the Life and Poetry of Donald Justice* (University of Iowa Press). He teaches at Lewis & Clark College in Portland, Oregon.

Harp writes: "As occurs on occasion with my poems, 'Houses' began with a line or two that appeared in a dream. It's difficult to say with precision what—if anything—gets translated from sleep into waking, but my impression is that something like the opening line was present when I woke up one morning. I repeated it many times before opening my eyes, for this moment of returning to wakefulness is often when my memories of dreams fade, if not shatter. Once I wrote down the opening lines, the rest of the poem followed rather quickly. As a matter of course, it underwent some revision, but its basic form was there from the start. Some of the circumstances of composition, such as the lounging cat, carried into the text.

"The poem recalls the abandoned houses that I saw, often when I was out running as a teenager, around the countryside of the southern Indiana where I grew up. One of these existed in our neighborhood on the edge of town and provided my childhood with a local image of the classic haunted house. Such mysterious places no doubt exist all over the world. I am counting on readers to bring their own experiences of such spaces to the poem. There is a powerful sense in which a text does not really exist until a reader connects with it and cocreates it by an act of reading. The poem makes a point of adverting explicitly to this textual situation."

JIM HARRISON was born in Grayling, Michigan, in 1937. He is the author of more than thirty-five books of poetry, nonfiction, and fiction. A member of the American Academy of Arts and Letters and winner of a Guggenheim Fellowship, he has had work published in twenty-five languages. His most recent works are *The English Major* (novel, Grove Press, 2008) and *In Search of Small Gods* (poetry, Copper Canyon Press, 2009). He lives in Montana and Arizona.

Of "Sunday Discordancies," Harrison writes: "Sometimes you wake up and wonder how much negative capability you're going to need to get through the day. As a child I'd wake up happy and then it would occur to me that World War II was going on and my uncles Walter and Artie were out in the South Pacific getting shot at.

"'Sunday Discordancies' is one of those poems, rare for me, that come all at once. It is the usual vain attempt to balance what cannot be balanced. In the end I resent it that some nitwit figured out the number of heartbeats in life. Years ago an American Indian friend told me that life is actually seven times slower than the way we live it. Go figure."

DOLORES HAYDEN was born in New York City in 1945. She is a professor at Yale University, president-elect of the Urban History Association, and author of several books about the American landscape including *The Power of Place* (The MIT Press, 1995), *Building Suburbia* (Pantheon, 2003), and *A Field Guide to Sprawl* (W. W. Norton, 2004). Last year she gave the Phi Beta Kappa poem at Yale. She has received awards from the Poetry Society of America and the New England Poetry Club. Her most recent poetry collection is *American Yard* (David Robert Books, 2004). Her Web site is www.DoloresHayden.com.

Hayden writes: "'Grave Goods' was inspired by a marvelous Tang Dynasty camel displayed in the booth of Priestley & Ferraro, London dealers in Chinese art, at an Asian Art Fair in New York. The sculpture of a Bactrian camel about two feet high incorporated a driver in a conical hat, a young passenger facing backward, small animals, and a variety of trade goods. After the exhibit, I looked into the geography of the Silk Road across Central Asia. I used iambic pentameter to provide a steady rhythm for the complex details of the journey. I also learned more about the Chinese practice of burying grave goods to supply the deceased in the afterlife.

"'Grave Goods' is addressed to my beloved husband, Peter Marris, sociologist, novelist, and world traveler, who was ill at the time we saw the camel together and died the following year. You could say this poem is my first attempt to provision him. 'Things Not of This World,' a second poem dealing with grave goods in the form of a ceramic house, appeared in the *Yale Review* in 2007. These are the last poems in a new collection I am just completing, *Nymph, Dun, and Spinner*."

TERRANCE HAYES was born in Columbia, South Carolina, in 1971. He is the author of *Wind in a Box* (Penguin, 2006), *Hip Logic* (Penguin, 2002), and *Muscular Music* (Carnegie Mellon University Contemporary Classics, 2005, and Tia Chucha Press, 1999). He has received a Whiting Writers Award, the Kate Tufts Discovery Award, a National Poetry Series award, and a National Endowment for the Arts Fellowship. His poems have appeared in two previous *Best American Poetry* anthologies. He is a professor of creative writing at Carnegie Mellon University and lives in Pittsburgh, Pennsylvania, with his family.

Of "A House Is Not a Home," Hayes writes: "Though this poem runs fairly close to an autobiographical experience, it's the fictitious/fanciful moments that ring truest for me. I read that Franz Kafka worked for a while at the 'Worker's Accident Insurance Institute for the Kingdom of Bohemia.' That sounds like the *real* in sur*real*. Where, in a parallel universe, would the black Kafka work, if not the African-American Acoustic and Audiological Accident Insurance Institute? And this poem is of course an elegy for crooner Luther Vandross, who I know was more complicated than his music let on . . . And an apology. This poem is an apology to Ron. He didn't actually punch me. But he should have."

K. A. HAYS was born in Phoenixville, Pennsylvania, in 1980. She grew up in Downingtown, studied English literature at Bucknell and Oxford universities, and earned a degree in the literary arts at Brown. Her first poetry collection, *Dear Apocalypse* (Carnegie Mellon), was published in 2009.

Of "The Way of All the Earth," Hays writes: "It was March when I wrote this poem, and billions of flea-like insects were hopping and carousing in the snow all over the New Hampshire woods. I wanted to know what they were and why they seemed to be flourishing. This led me to a good book about how animals have evolved to survive the winter: Bernd Heinrich's *Winter World* (HarperCollins, 2003). Watching and reading about the actions of other living things often serve as a reminder of human vulnerability, as does, for that matter, religion. In the Old Testament, when Joshua says, 'I am going the way of all the earth,' I hear a man gracefully acknowledging that he is as temporary as everything else. In this poem, my concern with temporality and human frailty met the subject about which I had been reading. I imagined humans scrambling to dodge death the way turtles do in winter—sinking under the mud of a pond, or piling on top of one another in a river's trench. The flea-like insects that spawned a poem featuring the habits of turtles turned out to be called snow fleas. As I learned from Heinrich, they are a four-hundred-million-year-old species whose survival tactics, like those of the turtles, must really be quite good."

BOB HICOK was born in 1960 in Grand Ledge, Michigan, under a full moon but without werewolves. He is an associate professor at Virginia Tech. His most recent collection, *This Clumsy Living* (University of Pittsburgh Press, 2007), was awarded the Bobbitt Prize from the Library of Congress. He has received three Pushcart Prizes, a Guggenheim, and two NEA Fellowships, and his poetry has been selected for inclusion in five volumes of *The Best American Poetry*. No more numbers in this bio, I promise.

Of "Mum's the word," Hicok writes: "I just want to say hello to David Wagoner. Mostly to his poems. And thank you. And that when cutting a gravel cake, it's best to wear safety glasses, according to OSHA."

DANIEL HOFFMAN was born in New York City in 1923. In 1973–74 he held the appointment now designated Poet Laureate. His thirteenth book of verse, *The Whole Nine Yards: Longer Poems,* appeared this year from Louisiana State University Press, publisher also of *Beyond Silence: Selected Shorter Poems 1948–2003,* and *Darkening Water* (2002). His book-length poem *Brotherly Love* (repr. University of Pennsylvania Press, 2000) was a finalist for both the National Book Award and the National Book Critics Circle Award in 1982. Best known among his half-dozen critical studies is *Poe Poe Poe Poe Poe Poe Poe* (repr. LSU Press, 1998), a National Book Award finalist in 1973. He edited *Over the Summer Water* (Orchises Press, 2008), poems by his late wife, Elizabeth McFarland. Hoffman lives in Swarthmore, Pennsylvania, and on Cape Rosier in Maine.

Of "A Democratic Vista," Hoffman writes: "During the run-up to the 2008 election, when the tone of one campaign turned nasty with moose-droppings and racial and religious smears, I found myself thinking back forty years to when I was a panelist—Louis Simpson was another—at a rally entitled 'Poetry and the National Purpose.' This was really a protest against the Vietnam War: much rhetoric, a few poems, but the war went on. I was moved, recalling this, to think what a contrast there is between the idealism of Our Great Poet, who sometimes overshoots his mark, and the sleazy accusations and innuendos then on TV. I began describing an imaginary conference based on the one I dimly remembered. In the then abusive electoral climate I left the encomium to our great national election 'Open- / ended—,' not knowing how it would turn out.

"How reassuring that a plurality of Americans have validated Walt Whitman's idealism and mine. The poem dictated itself in a style I hoped would enclose and express Whitman's sensibility without imitation. I hope the rather rough blank verse does this."

RICHARD HOWARD was born in Cleveland, Ohio, in 1929. He teaches in the writing division of Columbia University's School of the Arts, and continues against all odds to translate works of literature from the French. The most recent of his fifteen books of poems, *Without Saying,* was published in 2008 by Turtle Point Press. He was the guest editor of *The Best American Poetry 1995.*

Of "Arthur Englander's Back in School," Richard Howard writes: "This poem was the first or second of what has turned out to be a series of twelve of similar length and design, addressed in most cases to their principal, Mrs. Masters, by the dozen students of the fifth-grade class of Park School, an institute of progressive education in Sandusky, Ohio. I have been ensnared by their propositions and protests, and in order to round off or at least blunt the sequence that has taken over my existence, I have had to invite Mrs. Masters to bid farewell to the fifth-grade class and welcome its members to the sixth grade, rather a different proposition, as she will explain to them. I was, in actual fact, a member of this precocious colloquy, and have endeavored to record the truth of some of these Midwestern occasions, though the circumstances are rather archaic, biographically speaking, and I have had to imagine certain completory details. Still, as Arthur Englander would say, what's the difference between what you remember and what you make up? As the sequence has advanced, I am convinced that there is none. But I was by no means the most truthful member of the fifth grade at Park School."

P. HURSHELL was born in Seattle, Washington, several lives ago, in 1930. After studying at Boston's New England Conservatory of Music, she went to Europe, where she spent twenty-seven years singing in German and Austrian opera houses, guesting as well at the opera houses of Spain and Switzerland, Seattle, Chicago, New York, and New Orleans. She married an American opera singer in Berlin, had two children in Vienna, and basically evolved into a rather cynical Central European whose favorite parts were Salome and Lulu. When she retired and came back to Seattle she enrolled at the University of Washington as an English major, fascinated by the American take on texts and cultures. She got her degrees in a leisurely fashion, reluctant to leave the academic dialogues; received a Woodrow Wilson and a Ford grant for her research on Jewish women and the Shoah; was awarded the Robert Heilman Distinguished Dissertation Award for *When Silence Speaks, When Women Sorrow* (1991); taught for the English and women's studies departments from 1978 to 1995; and has only recently begun to publish her poetry. Besides working on her poetry manuscript *Outside the Commentaries,* she is also translating the German Shoah poets Gertrude Kolmar, Hilde Donin, and Rose Ausländer. She currently edits, gets bossy in grassroots politics, belongs to a Hebrew texts study group, and gives an occasional workshop on women and their Shoah resistances. She is a member of the Wallingford Irregulars, a Seattle poetry workshop; and a participant in Richard Hugo House poetry workshops.

Of "In Winter," Hurshell writes: "This poem began with its various parts all far from one another: the dead bird in the fog, the Hanukkah season, what the possible metaphysics of that season might be. One day I came across Ginsberg's 'Psalm III' and admired its blend of political hard rap and the 'visionary.' It's crystal-clear, etched but never harsh. It gave me an angle or a bit of a shove to work on. I tried to keep my lines as understated and quiet as possible, in rather fugue-like fashion. I always depend on sound-on-the-breath's rhythms for line breaks, and aside from whatever motif-focus is going on, I like to play with the speaker's voice—is this an aria, an ensemble, a duet, a cadenza? I think of 'In Winter' as an ensemble piece with a solo cello."

MICHAEL JOHNSON was born in Bella Coola, British Columbia, in 1978. His family lived as missionaries in the eastern highlands of Zaïre when he was young, and the memories have never left him. He grew up around mountains and wildlife and books, studied field biology in Idaho, and received a BA in creative writing from Lewis-Clark State College. He lives in Vancouver, and works for Vancouver Wine Vault, cellaring private wine collections. "How to Be Eaten by a Lion" is the title poem of his first manuscript.

Of "How to Be Eaten by a Lion," Johnson writes: "I wrote this poem waiting for a biology class to start. I was twenty and hell-bent, sometimes skipping classes to write, sometimes not realizing I'd missed them at all. It started with just a voice in my head, cheeky as you will, sort of a wildlife documentary narrator, and it was simply a title: 'How to Be Eaten by a Lion.' (I might have been heavily into Monty Python at the time.) There was a pomp and aloofness to the voice, and I managed it for about a line before the poem turned serious and took the reins. I'm pretty sure I had read Philip Levine's 'They Feed They Lion' about thirty times that weekend, and the poem came easily. It took fifteen minutes. Class started without me. My professor must have recognized my rapture in the back corner and didn't interrupt. I've always been grateful for that. I usually revise a lot, yet this piece has remained almost unchanged. Something about the poem led me to keep sending it, very jealously at first, to the best magazines I could think of. It ended up getting turned down over fifty times, though often with nice notes. Friends keep asking why it takes so long to get some poems published, and I tell them it's a mystery. Some days a poem consumes you—writer, reader; some days you're just *that* lucky."

TINA KELLEY was born in Dover, New Jersey, in 1963. She is a reporter for the *New York Times.* Her first poetry book, *The Gospel of Galore* (Word Press, Cincinnati), won a 2003 Washington State Book Award. She contributed to the *Times* reporting on the September 11 attacks, and wrote 121 "Portraits of Grief," small obituaries about the victims, as part of the team that won a Pulitzer Prize for public service. Her poems have appeared in the *Journal of the American Medical Association, Southwest Review, Poetry Northwest, Prairie Schooner,* and the *Beloit Poetry Journal,* among other publications, and on the buses of Seattle, Washington. She lives in Maplewood, New Jersey, with her husband and their two children.

Kelley writes: "This poem, 'To Yahweh,' owes its existence to the hours I spend reading, in search of serendipity. The epigraph came from a selection of my book club, *weequashing* surfaced during some quality time with the *Oxford English Dictionary,* and the fire darkening down is how firefighters talk, overheard on my late-night rewrite shift at the *Times.* The whisper song came from the Audubon bird encyclopedia, curing mice in a cello was a delightful bit found online while researching the cello I was learning to play, and the acrid or burned quality of space came from an article in the *Atlantic* by William Langeweische.

"And that weird sexuality of wild bird rehabilitators? That's from one of several lectures I've attended about falconry. Delightful surprises can arise anywhere.

"I collect these bits and wait for them to stick together, like pebbles in a puddingstone."

MAUD KELLY was born in St. Louis, Missouri, in 1973, and lives and teaches there. Her poems have most recently appeared in *Best New Poets 2006* and *American Literary Review*. She is currently finishing her first book of poetry.

On "What I Think of Death, If Anyone's Asking," Kelly writes: "Humans (shake of head). It's got to be really tiresome, I bet, if you're any other thing in nature, to witness our shenanigans. But we're so beautiful, too—the beauty of the bewildered, I guess I mean, of fairy-tale children lost in the woods who will hopefully find the bread-crumbs—so I try to write poems that sympathize with us a little bit. And in the Irish tradition, I'm interested in shame. Strange thing, isn't it? On the one hand, it can be terribly disconnecting, a thing that makes us feel far away and like we'll never be worth much. On the other hand, we *do* sometimes do shameful things, and the ability to acknowledge that truth, and beyond that, to really feel its weight, seems kind of essential to bringing us closer to understanding ourselves, so there's some sweetness in it, too."

LANCE LARSEN was born in Pocatello, Idaho, in 1961. He received his PhD from the University of Houston and now teaches at Brigham Young University. He has written three books of poems: *Backyard Alchemy* (Tampa, 2009), *In All Their Animal Brilliance* (Tampa, 2005), and *Erasable Walls* (New Issues, 1998). He has received a Pushcart Prize and a 2007 fellowship from the National Endowment for the Arts. In 2009 he codirected a theater study abroad program in London.

Of "Why do you keep putting animals in your poems?" Larsen writes: "At our house we have a mongrel Abyssinian, a bearded dragon, three basement tarantulas, half a dozen deer that use our backyard as a Motel 6, and a gorgeous but deceased lovebird in the freezer awaiting proper burial once the ground thaws. In short, animal life presses in. How can I not, at least once in a while, try to channel that energy? With this poem, the title came first, a magnetic north toward which ensuing sentences pointed. I felt myself nudged forward by wonder, and found that what I'd written was an undercover ode to creatures furred and feathered—and a paean to our own animal mystery."

PHILLIS LEVIN was born in Paterson, New Jersey, in 1954, and educated at Sarah Lawrence College and Johns Hopkins University. She has written four volumes of poetry, *Temples and Fields* (University of Georgia Press, 1988), *The Afterimage* (Copper Beech Press, 1995), *Mercury* (Penguin, 2001), and *May Day* (Penguin, 2008), and is the editor of *The Penguin Book of the Sonnet* (Penguin, 2001). She has received the Poetry Society of America's 1988 Norma Farber First Book Award, a 1995 Fulbright Scholar Award to Slovenia, the 1999 Amy Lowell Poetry Traveling Scholarship (which she spent living in Italy), a 2003 Guggenheim Fellowship, and a 2007 National Endowment for the Arts Fellowship. She lives in New York, is a professor of English and poet-in-residence at Hofstra University, and also teaches in the graduate creative writing program at New York University.

Levin writes: "'Open Field' originated while I was crossing a field at dawn to get breakfast after intense scrutiny of the role of commas in a group of poems by John Donne. I heard the first lines in my head the moment I saw a cluster of crows, some in the trees, some on the grass. They seemed to punctuate the landscape. The day before I started this poem I had just finished correcting the final set of proofs for my anthology, *The Penguin Book of the Sonnet,* when my editor called to say I needed to address a few more queries, one of which concerned the highly eccentric punctuation in the sonnets by Donne I had selected. The versions that I chose and strongly preferred, all from Sir Herbert J. C. Grierson's edition, did not correspond with those published in *The Norton Anthology of Poetry,* so I was asked to revisit my decision. I was up to my eyebrows in commas, thinking about how Donne deployed them so generously in some cases, so parsimoniously in others. But reconsidering those commas, even the oddest ones, only intensified my sense that they articulated Donne's instinct for performance—the artful pause and the natural breath—and his counterpointing the drama of speech with the rhythm of thought. What had annoyed me most, though, in the Norton edition was a comma inserted after 'Death' in the opening line of 'Death be not proud'—which seemed to interrupt the momentum, dissipate the tension, and undercut the tone. In the version edited by Grierson, the only comma in that line falls after 'proud' ('Death be not proud, though some have callèd thee'). In many other places in the Grierson edition, commas that our modern rules of syntax deem unnecessary or plain wrong added rhetorical force or a subtle undercurrent to the argument. But none of this was on my mind any longer: I was simply crossing a field, trying to get to breakfast. The release from the burden of editing that anthology and the act of holding my ground, standing up for a decision I believed in, as well as the freedom to write poems again, provoked immense joy."

PHILIP LEVINE was born in Detroit in 1928. He was educated at the public schools and at Wayne University (now Wayne State), then the city university of Detroit. At age twenty-six he left Detroit for other pastures, and the city slowly collapsed (there is "no connection although I also slowly collapsed"). His eighteenth collection, *News of the World,* will appear in September 2009. He has won the Pulitzer, National Book Critics Circle Award, and National Book Award. He lives half the year in Fresno, where he taught for twenty-two years, half in Brooklyn.

Of "Words on the Wind," Levine writes: "I wrote the first draft of the poem in the summer of 2003 after hearing odd words out of nowhere, but it wasn't until January of 2008 I got a version I wanted to publish. The site of the poem: Dearborn—the factory town that served Ford—was like its master, Henry, notoriously racist & anti-Semitic. (I've no idea what it's like now.) In 1952 I had a job driving a truck for an outfit in Detroit that repaired electric motors. Twice a week I'd drive out to the great Rouge plant to pick up or deliver a gigantic motor; it was at least an hour each way, which meant I was out of the shop for the whole morning; I loved that part. But I hated the drive inside the factory: Sometimes I had to back in between men & machines for what seemed like hundreds of yards to where the motor was deposited by a crane onto the truck bed. I'd discovered this grassy, undeveloped area a few miles east of the factory, & on the way back when the weather was decent I'd reward myself & take my lunch up to a wild knoll & dine in solitude. And of course I would meditate on my life, which at the time was a mess—bad marriage, a job with no future, & a need no one else respected: to write poetry. I was even less spiritual then than I am now: I believed in wood, stone, iron, flesh, grass, but I also believed in the magic of words, though as yet not my own words, but certainly the ones that came to me on the wind."

SARAH LINDSAY was born in Cedar Rapids, Iowa, in 1958. She is the author of *Primate Behavior* (Grove Press Poetry Series, 1997, a finalist for the National Book Award), *Mount Clutter* (Grove Press Poetry Series, 2002), and *Twigs and Knucklebones* (Copper Canyon Press, 2008). A graduate of St. Olaf College and the UNC-Greensboro MFA program in creative writing, she apprenticed for a few years at Unicorn Press, learning to set type, and print and bind books by hand. She works as a copyeditor and proofreader at Pace Communications, Inc., in Greensboro, North Carolina. She plays the cello with friends in a quartet that is sometimes a trio or quintet, and lives with her husband and their small dog among toppling piles of books and papers in Greensboro.

Of "Tell the Bees," Lindsay writes: "When I come across something that I need to use in a poem, my mind snags on it. I don't have a better verb for it, but the sensation is satisfactory. The inside of my head sits up straighter; it becomes eager. It sends a hand to a pen: Time for a note.

"A snag like this occurred when I read about the tradition of informing domestic bees of events, such as births and deaths, in the keeper's household. This gave me a way to think about what I'd been thinking about. I had come back from my father's funeral to my home in a city where no one else knew him, no one else knew to grieve. I don't keep bees, but I could pass along the instructions."

THOMAS LUX was born in Northampton, Massachusetts, in 1946. He is the Bourne Professor of Poetry at the Georgia Institute of Technology. His most recent books, both from Houghton Mifflin, are *God Particles* (2008) and *The Cradle Place* (2004).

JOANIE MACKOWSKI was born in 1963 and grew up in Connecticut. She teaches at the University of Cincinnati; she previously worked as a French translator, a trucking industry reporter, and a juggler. Her books of poems are *View from a Temporary Window* (Pitt Poetry Series, 2009) and *The Zoo* (Pitt Poetry Series, 2002).

Of "Boarding: *Hemaris thysbe*," Mackowski writes: "I love hummingbird moths; they're mind-blowing to watch. And in *Speak, Memory*, Nabokov has a passage about mimicry in nature, about instances when an insect's or butterfly's 'protective device was carried to a point of mimetic subtlety, exuberance, and luxury far in excess of a predator's power of appreciation.' This idea of accidental artistic mastery is also mind-blowing to me, but it's not really what the poem's about. The poem's about floating or drowning in a sea of appearances."

CHRISTINE MARSHALL was born in Santa Monica, California, in 1974. She is a doctoral fellow at the University of Utah. Her manuscript, *Fits of White,* is currently seeking publication.

Of "Sweat," Marshall writes: "I am interested in how certain repulsive aspects of our bodies, reframed, become necessary, even beautiful. Sweat is an obvious example of this transformation: full of toxins, it is also a chance at renewal. When I tell the story of working out at the gym and hearing a man say that he thinks it's gross when girls sweat, I hear a range of responses, from 'I think it's gross when anyone sweats' to 'Sweat is a turn-on.' I appreciate the friction of these different perspectives, the way they bump up against each other and produce new tensions; I also appreciate language that works as hard as the body can: words that grunt and flex and reach."

CLEOPATRA MATHIS was born in Ruston, Louisiana, in 1947, and was raised there by her Greek family. Her first book, *Aerial View of Louisiana*, was published in 1979 by Sheep Meadow, followed by *The Bottom Land* (1983), *The Center for Cold Weather* (1989), *Guardian* (1995), and *What to Tip the Boatman?* (2001). Sarabande Books published her sixth book, *White Sea,* in 2005. Since 1982, she has taught at Dartmouth College, where she is the Frederick Sessions Beebe '35 Professor in the Art of Writing.

Of "Canis," Mathis writes: "Every sentence in this poem is true, which made the writing of it a kind of gift. It all happened: the coyotes' mysterious arrival on the outer beach of Provincetown on Cape Cod; the shack out there in the dunes where my then-husband and I were staying, our stupid argument, our misunderstanding of each other made manifest in the noise we heard, the black humor of it."

J. D. McCLATCHY (born 1945) has recently edited *The Whole Difference: Selected Writings of Hugo von Hofmannsthal* (Princeton), *The Four Seasons* (Knopf), and, with Stephen Yenser, a *Selected Poems* by James Merrill (Knopf). The Metropolitan Opera has issued a DVD of his English adaptation of Mozart's *The Magic Flute,* and Knopf published his sixth collection of poems, *Mercury Dressing,* earlier this year. He teaches at Yale, where he also edits the *Yale Review,* and is president of the American Academy of Arts and Letters. He lives in Stonington, Connecticut.

Of "Lingering Doubts," McClatchy writes: "Poems accumulate—or mine tend to. Tremulous globules . . . an image, a phrase, a feeling . . . begin to condense on the pane of a larger idea. Proximity encourages their combination into something larger, moister, more glistening. Even so, there are times when some bead or other doesn't join, is left at the edge. Most are then merely shaken off. Sometimes, one is transferred to the notebook, a note too sharp or flat to go with the rest. I noticed a few of these and strung them together as 'Lingering Doubts,' the title pointing to their common occasion. I might have let each stand on its own, but the age of the epigram seems to have passed with J. V. Cunningham. Hence this small suite of doubts, their tone of voice shifting from the ironic to the embittered to the plaintive."

W. S. MERWIN was born in New York City in 1927. He was educated at Princeton. From 1949 to 1951 he worked as a tutor in France, Portugal, and Majorca, later earning his living by translating from the French, Spanish, Latin, and Portuguese. About those early years, Merwin told Ben George of *Fugue* magazine that he "mainly had a hand-to-mouth existence for years. I worked as a tutor, and you didn't make much money doing that. Then I went to England and I lived on what I earned from the BBC, which wasn't very much, but enough to manage to live. It didn't take much money. So I just kept that going as long as I could. I kept thinking, It'll come to an end and I'll have to go to a university. But year after year it didn't. And then I got a few fellowships. . . . My models were people who lived on very little money, who assumed that if you were a writer or a composer or something like that you didn't have much money. Maybe later on in your life you had a bit. But you took it for granted that you'd have no money. It didn't seem important." *A Mask for Janus,* Merwin's first book of poems, was chosen by W. H. Auden as the 1952 volume in the Yale Series of Younger Poets. Recent collections include *Present Company* (Copper Canyon, 2007), *Migration: New & Selected Poems* (2005), which won the 2005 National Book Award, and *The Pupil* (2002). His new book is *The Shadow of Sirius* (Copper Canyon Press, 2008). He lives in Haiku, Hawaii.

Of "The Silence of the Mine Canaries," Merwin writes: "I remember wanting to see birds when I was a child in Union City, New Jersey, and being told that the birds I saw in the bird book I was given were somewhere else. Part of my disappointment, I realize now, was that no one else seemed to care that some of those birds had lived where we were living, and were not there any more. Both feelings—the spontaneous attraction to birds, and the regret at their absence—their growing absence—as well as the disappointment at the general indifference to them, stayed with me through the years. In France, the actual place where I have lived for parts of my life since the 1950s, is a region where the birds of northern and southern Europe have both lived. In a small section of oak woods, in the early '60s, I identified over a hundred and fifty species one summer. Many of them I have never seen again. I do not think this can be reversed. I think human beings have caused it, and I think it is part of a progression from which we are not separate. Perhaps the most shocking single detail, to me, was the sudden absence, one year, of the swallows that had come every spring, nested there, and gathered all day and especially at evening, on the telephone wire above the village square. Everyone saw them and heard them, and when they did not come at all, no one seemed to notice. It is indeed a poem of mourning."

JUDE NUTTER was born North Yorkshire, England, in 1960, and grew up near Hanover in northern Germany. She holds a BA in printmaking (Winchester School of Art, England) and an MFA in poetry (University of Oregon, Eugene). Her first collection, *Pictures of the Afterlife* (Salmon Poetry, Ireland), was published in 2002. *The Curator of Silence* (University of Notre Dame Press), her second collection, won the 2007 Minnesota Book Award in Poetry. Her third collection, *I Wish I Had a Heart Like Yours, Walt Whitman* (University of Notre Dame Press) was published in 2009. In 2004 she spent two months in Antarctica as a participant in the National Science Foundation's Writers and Artists Program. She has lived in Minnesota since 1998 and teaches at the Loft Literary Center and at various other venues in the Twin Cities.

Nutter writes: "As a child, I was an avid insect collector, and 'The Insect Collector's Demise' explores the shift I made, in my early teens, away from my killing jars and nets. Even though I am British by birth, I grew up in Germany, and the house I grew up in was taken over by the Waffen SS in early 1945 and incorporated into the Bergen-Belsen concentration camp. Camp records reveal that 869 Polish Jews, Gypsies, and 'others' were interred in this building. Needless to say, as I grew older and began to grasp just what had happened at Bergen-Belsen, my feelings about my hobby of insect collecting began to change. With the typical magical thinking of a young girl, I began to equate my killing hundreds of insects with the mass deaths at Bergen-Belsen. I eventually abandoned my killing jars and nets, but the insect collector remains an evocative figure for me: one that represents both childhood innocence and the terrible destruction such innocence enables."

SHARON OLDS was born in San Francisco, California, in 1942. Her most recent books are *One Secret Thing* (Knopf, 2008) and *Strike Sparks: Selected Poems, 1980–2002* (Knopf, 2004). She teaches at New York University and lives in New York City.

Olds writes: "When I looked for 'Self-Exam,' to say a few words about it here, I found it in the middle part of *One Secret Thing,* following a poem with the falling off of an umbilical cord (umbilical chord?) in it, and one with the nap time of a nursing baby, and others with a tooth fairy, a diaphragm, a dress borrowed by someone (the poem's speaker's daughter) off to college, and an elderly mother's (the speaker's mother's!) toxic shock and recovery. It was fun for me to see the poem in its sort of chronological context.

"Several things come to mind. First, a conversation with someone not a poetry reader, someone very smart, who had not understood the ending of 'Self-Exam'—and my attempt to be sort of hearty and unembarrassing in response, saying that I saw it as the speaker of the poem (ah, that speaker!) remembering making love.

"Second, now that I'm working on a new collection, *Stag's Leap, Poems 1997–2000*—an end-of-long-marriage book—I see that this poem was written around the time of those turn-of-the-century poems, in a voice of elegy as well as (almost a kind of magic realism?) descriptive frenzy!

"So finally there is a third thing to say, because I'm pretty amazed to see that there are no similes here, it's all metaphor—whereas often my poems seem anxious about the extent of the 'transformative claim' in metaphor, seeming more comfortable with the more literal-minded 'like.'"

MARY OLIVER was born in the Cleveland suburb of Maple Heights in 1935. She has published fifteen books of poetry and five books of prose. *American Primitive* received the Pulitzer Prize in 1984, and *New and Selected Poems* won the National Book Award in 1992. Beacon Press published *New and Selected Poems, Volume Two* in 2005 as well as her first poetry CD, *At Blackwater Pond,* in 2006. *Red Bird,* her most recent book, was published by Beacon Press in 2008. She has lived in Provincetown, Massachusetts, for more than forty years.

Oliver writes: "'Red' is simply a true narrative, and I felt it should be told simply. I'm very conscious of adjectives; I call them the 'nickel' words and in some poems I offer a lot of nickels. But in this poem I thought they would only modify the scene, so there is only one, used twice, which is of course the word 'death.'"

LINDA PASTAN grew up in New York City, graduated from Radcliffe College, and received an MA from Brandeis University. She has published twelve volumes of poetry, most recently *Queen of a Rainy Country.* Two of her books have been finalists for the National Book Award. She has been poet laureate of Maryland, and in 2003 she won the Ruth Lilly Poetry Prize for lifetime achievement. She lives with her husband in Potomac, Maryland. They have three children and seven grandchildren.

Of "Insomnia," Pastan writes: "When insomnia strikes, I often fight the boredom of those empty hours by writing poems in my head—and what better subject than insomnia itself?"

KEVIN PRUFER was born in Cleveland, Ohio, in 1969. He is the author of several poetry collections, including *National Anthem* (Four Way Books, 2008), *Fallen from a Chariot* (Carnegie Mellon, 2005), and *The Finger Bone* (Carnegie Mellon, 2002). He is also coeditor of *New European Poets* (Graywolf, 2008) and *Pleiades: A Journal of New Writing*. He has also published mystery stories in *Alfred Hitchcock's Mystery Magazine* and *Crimewave* (UK). His next book is forthcoming from Four Way Books. He lives in Warrensburg, Missouri.

Of "On Mercy," Prufer writes: "My father grew up in Germany before and during the Second World War, immigrated to this country in the 1950s, and worked as a professional archaeologist and amateur classical historian. I grew up surrounded by artifacts of that war, by older bones, stone tools, ancient coins, the bits and pieces of vanished societies. His interests have continued in my own poetry, much of which takes place in a sort of imagined past, during imagined or real wars, often in several times and historical settings simultaneously. The setting of 'On Mercy' is mostly imaginary, though I suppose conversations with my father about the war influenced it (the absurdity of the opening scene, of the victim's body being dragged through town and out to a field). Although I worry that saying so might oversimplify the poem, one of the questions I think about as I write is this: After so many generations of increasing war and cruelty, have we really earned anyone's forgiveness? The bullets and gold fillings strung on a chain at the end of the poem seem to me a pretty sorry sort of mercy."

SUSAN BLACKWELL RAMSEY was born in Detroit in 1950, graduated from Kalamazoo College in 1972, and has managed to live in Kalamazoo most of the time since. When the independent bookstore she worked in closed in 2004, she was fortunate enough to be accepted into Notre Dame's MFA program, graduating in 2008. Her work was featured in Wayne State University's *New Poems from the Third Coast: Contemporary Michigan Poetry*. In 2007 she won the Marjorie J. Wilson Award from *Margie: The American Journal of Poetry*.

Of "Pickled Heads: St. Petersburg," Ramsey writes: "When I read Stephen J. Asma's *Stuffed Animals and Pickled Heads: The Culture and Evolution of Natural History Museums,* I was intrigued by his account of the role of 'spirits of wine' in specimen preservation. In my day it was possible for a natural-born English major to graduate from high school without taking chemistry, so the process of distilling 'spirits of wine' was news to me. Asma didn't give nearly enough details for my taste, though, about those heads Peter preserved, so I started nosing around.

"I have the kind of mind that retains only inessential information. Those two heads nudged a memory of the Murrieta head in Antonio Banderas's *The Mask of Zorro,* of the travels of Eva Perón's corpse in Tomás Eloy Martinez's *Santa Evita,* of an old *Horizon* article showing Jeremy Bentham in his cabinet with a caption to explain that the head we see is wax, that the real head is in the bottom drawer. While I confirmed facts, was sidetracked by details, and besieged by coincidences (for my purposes it was almost too good that a man named Love claimed to have killed Murrieta), I had time to wonder about our penchant for preservation, our touching and sometimes grotesque need to make things last."

KEITH RATZLAFF was born in Henderson, Nebraska, in 1953. He is the author of two poetry chapbooks, *Out Here* (State Street Press, 1984) and *New Winter Light* (Nightshade Press, 1994), as well as four books of poetry, *Man Under a Pear Tree* (Anhinga Press, 1997), *Across the Known World* (Loess Hills Press, 1997), *Dubious Angels: Poems after Paul Klee* (Anhinga Press, 2005), and *Then, a Thousand Crows* (Anhinga Press, 2009). He teaches writing at Central College in Pella, Iowa.

Ratzlaff writes: "'Turn'—like many of my recent poems—brings together a number of unrelated things: my old cat; a wooden statue of a woman on a donkey I keep on a bookshelf; a bone I picked up on a walk by the river; the fact that the word 'vertebra' comes from the Indo-European root 'to turn'; a news story about a man in a southern Iowa town. Although I've taken a few liberties with his story (not the least of which is moving the incident to my home town, Pella—where, of course, nothing like this would ever take place), mostly things happened as they are described in the poem. The house was a minor tourist attraction for a while; the quoted lines in the poem were literally spray-painted on the siding, and I copied them verbatim."

ADRIENNE RICH was born in Baltimore, Maryland, in 1929. She has lived in New York, New England, and, since 1984, California. Her most recent books of poetry are *Fox* (2001), *The School Among the Ruins* (2004), and *Telephone Ringing in the Labyrinth* (2007). Her collections of essays include *Arts of the Possible* (2001), *What Is Found There: Notebooks on Poetry and Politics* (1993, 2003), and *A Human Eye: Essays on Art in Society* (forthcoming in 2009), all from W. W. Norton & Co. She was the guest editor of *The Best American Poetry 1996.*

Rich writes: "I hope 'Tonight No Poetry Will Serve' needs no gloss."

JAMES RICHARDSON was born in Bradenton, Florida, in 1950 and grew up in Garden City, New York. His recent books include *Interglacial: New and Selected Poems and Aphorisms* (Ausable, 2004), which was a finalist for the National Book Critics Circle Award, *Vectors: Aphorisms and Ten-Second Essays* (Ausable, 2001), and *How Things Are* (Carnegie Mellon, 2000). He has received an Award in Literature from the American Academy of Arts and Letters. He is professor of creative writing and English at Princeton University. "Subject, Verb, Object" is included in *By the Numbers,* which will be published by Copper Canyon in 2010.

Of "Subject, Verb, Object," Richardson writes: "The first two stanzas are straight linguistics and prosody, the third something I've always felt, that trying to control a proliferation of *I*-sounds in a strict line was like lassoing air. As for the fourth, well, I routinely walk to work, six miles round trip, and whether on Sunday or Thursday or Tuesday often see the kind of Sunday jogger who ran into the poem and finally finished it for me."

PATTIANN ROGERS was born in Joplin, Missouri, in 1940. She graduated Phi Beta Kappa from the University of Missouri in 1961 and received a master of arts degree from the University of Houston in 1981. She has published thirteen books, including *Wayfare* (Penguin, 2008), *Firekeeper* (revised and expanded ed., Milkweed Editions, 2005), *Generations* (Penguin, 2004), and *Song of the World Becoming, New and Collected Poems, 1981–2001* (Milkweed Editions, 2001). She has received two NEA grants, a Guggenheim Fellowship, a 2005 Literary Award in Poetry from the Lannan Foundation, and five Pushcart Prizes. She spent the spring of 2000 in residence at the Rockefeller Foundation's Study and Conference Center in Bellagio, Italy. She has taught as a visiting professor at various universities, including the Universities of Texas, Arkansas, and Montana, and at Washington University. Rogers has two sons and three grandsons and lives with her husband, a retired geophysicist, in Colorado.

Rogers writes: "As with most poems, many threads from various sources and experiences came together as the origin of 'A Blind Astronomer in the Age of Stars.' I couldn't list or even understand all of them. But I know three of them. One was the term 'Age of Stars,' which struck me as having a depth of implication about time and existence that was ominous and exhilarating. It suggested a before and an after to the time of stars, our time, all those stars surrounding us, including our sun, their light coming into being and then disappearing. What kind of blackness would that be? Secondly, I had for years been intrigued by Helen Keller's claim that she could feel moonlight. I had tried often, closing my eyes, to feel that light myself. Then, I have maintained an interest in astronomy that began years ago with a course I took as an undergraduate. I had just watched a long lecture series on the subject shortly before beginning this poem.

"Starting from these origins and from my experiences of being close to the feel and fragrances of the earth at night beneath the stars, I began the poem, creating a character, a blind astronomer, to help me examine aspects of our perceptions of the stars and our stance in the universe. The writing of the poem was the process of making my way through the wonder of it all."

GIBBONS RUARK was born in Raleigh, North Carolina, in 1941, and grew up in various Methodist parsonages in the eastern part of the state. Educated at the universities of North Carolina and Massachusetts, he taught English largely at the University of Delaware until his retirement in 2005. He has published his poems widely for over forty years. Among his eight collections are *Keeping Company* (Johns Hopkins, 1983), *Passing Through Customs: New and Selected Poems* (LSU, 1999), and *Staying Blue*, a 2008 chapbook from Lost Hills Books of Duluth, Minnesota. The recipient of many awards, including three NEA Poetry Fellowships, a Pushcart Prize, and the 1984 Saxifrage Prize for *Keeping Company,* he lives with his wife, Kay, in Raleigh.

Of "John Clare's Finches," Ruark writes: "The beginning and ending of this poem lay around separately for a very long time, like the panels of a diptych that haven't found their hinge. I had the first nine lines about watching goldfinches with my wife and the last eleven about John Clare having simply walked out of an insane asylum to roam the countryside looking for his first love Mary Joyce, refusing to believe that she had died. Then suddenly I realized one day that the goldfinch in line seventeen was a link to the finches at the start, and just as suddenly I had the line 'And they came, but on a wind that never blew before,' and I knew it was the hinge on which my diptych could fold, or, if you will, unfold."

JOHN RYBICKI was born in Detroit, Michigan, in 1961, grew up there, and currently teaches at Alma College. He also works with Wings of Hope Hospice teaching poetry writing to children who have gone through a trauma or loss. This past year his wife, the poet Julie Moulds, died after a valiant sixteen-year battle with cancer. Rybicki is the author of three books of poems, *Traveling at High Speeds* (New Issues Poetry and Prose, 2003), *Yellow-Haired Girl with Spider* (March Street Press, 2002), and his latest collection, *We Bed Down into Water,* which was published by Northwestern University Press in 2008.

Of "This Tape Measure Made of Light," Rybicki writes: "In the context of the heavens and earth, as physical objects, we are minutiae. Yet the human spirit—that giant of ours—is vast beyond naming. You would need *a tape measure made of light* to measure our spiritual proportions. Poetry is the language of our largeness (spirit) and the language of our brokenness.

"As a poet I've taken up the war club of the pry bar (working at a tire shop) and hammer (doing construction). I flat-out love physical work. It acts as a healthy counterbalance to the creative parts of my nature—that self who is always banging his head against the heavens. And I just don't travel well. On the occasion of this poem, I joined a new work crew and labored in some far land with strangers. My beloved wife, who knows how freaked out I get about traveling, wrapped me in gauze, but out the door I went, fear or no fear.

"Still, so many of the idiosyncrasies and fascinations I have as a poet meld or whirl around in this poem. We were building a structure with precise proportions even as my spirit felt like it was ripping through my skin and wanting out. I wore the mask of a hyper but hardworking laborer with these men, and felt lucky to be dunked in such a fascinating environment as a feed mill for animals. But I was scared half shitless. There was a fine powdery dust flying everywhere and I have a pretty serious case of asthma. At lunch when I climbed down through this hatch in the ceiling, this young man with earmuffs on just looked up at me and nodded and I drank that moment of human contact and fellowship. It helped quell the terror a little.

"My wife was my deep earth in a frenetic world. I have a little card Julie gave me when my breathing carried me home to her after that first day of carpentry. She didn't kick my ass around the block for my strange vulnerabilities. She wrote in the box 'I am right here. I am always with you my Dude.' Then she drew a picture of herself with a heart for a body between her hips and throat and I carried the card with me the next day when I went off into battle again.

"P.S.: change change change. Everything's always in flux. We grow to become a collage of ourselves. The body is a kind of factory replicating in incremental fashion new selves over and over again. We are relentlessly becoming, aren't we? The poet John Woods writes, 'I want to take my own hand, and in a still place in the wind, be what I have become.' I say amen to that. What I added to this discourse in the poem is this: 'The pictures on our driver's licenses should be liquid and ever changing.' I say amen to that as well."

BETSY SHOLL was born in Lakewood, Ohio, in 1945. She is the author of seven collections of poetry, most recently *Rough Cradle* (Alice James Books, 2009), and *Late Psalm* (University of Wisconsin, 2004). She has received fellowships from the National Endowment for the Arts and the Maine Arts Commission, and is currently poet laureate of Maine. She teaches at the University of Southern Maine and the Vermont College of Fine Arts.

Of "Gravity and Grace," Sholl writes: "This poem grew out of my reading of Simone Weil, and I have to admit the poem required much labor. Early on, the playground boys presented a helpful counterbalance to Weil's greater severity. Many times, however, I had to put the poem aside, for inability to get closer to Weil's sensibility, to arrive at a closure that didn't seem forced. But always I was drawn back—to the poem and to Weil herself, trying to honor her complexity and pathos, her almost palpable presence in the very words she wanted destroyed."

MARTHA SILANO was born in New Jersey in 1961. She graduated from Metuchen High School and received her BA from Grinnell College. After stints as a farm laborer, CPS caseworker, and legal secretary, she studied poetry at the University of Washington (MFA, 1993). She is the author of *Blue Positive* (Steel Toe Books, 2006) and *What the Truth Tastes Like* (Nightshade Press, 1999). She teaches at Bellevue College, near her home in Seattle, Washington, where she resides with her husband, writer Langdon Cook, and their two children.

Silano writes: "'Love' began during a freewrite with my beginning poetry students. It was time to get past the moon/June/croon syndrome, so I announced we'd be experimenting with the other end of the spectrum. Tonight's assignment: Write a poem of address modeled on Julie Sheehan's 'Hate Poem' [which Paul Muldoon selected for *The Best American Poetry 2005*]. I remember laughing hard that night and saying 'Yes! Good!' quite a bit as they shared their fresh and lively drafts. I tucked my own into a drawer, but when I came across it a year later, I couldn't help but tinker. The anger that had fueled the initial draft had cooled, so it was easier to be objective—to pick and choose my images, focus on pacing, to cut away all but the essential. It's not exactly a poem I want to be remembered by, nor is it especially representative of my work, but I am pleased with how it turned out. And my husband? He's still trying to figure out what's so bad about his knees."

MITCH SISSKIND was born in Chicago in 1945. "I've lived in Los Angeles since 1986 but still feel Chicago is my home. In 1984 Brightwaters Press published *Visitations,* a book of my stories, and in 1993 WiseAcre Books published *Dog Man Stories,* three tales of pit bulls. Beginning also in 1993 I edited seven issues of the *Stud Duck,* a magazine about pit bulls, entrepreneurship, and imaginative writing. The relentless energy of pit bulls attracted and inspired me and I found it easy to write about them, though I've actually met very few pit bulls."

Sisskind writes: "My poem 'Like a Monkey' is based on a midrashic commentary in which rabbis debate the relative beauty of three women—and one man—from the book of Genesis. This was the first poem I'd written in many years, and I owe it to being once more in the presence of my old college chums at a Columbia University reunion."

TOM SLEIGH was born in Mount Pleasant, Texas. His most recent book of poetry, *Space Walk* (Houghton Mifflin, 2007), won the 2008 Kingsley Tufts Award. His book of essays, *Interview with a Ghost,* was published by Graywolf Press in 2006. He has also published *After One* (Houghton Mifflin, 1983), *Waking* (University of Chicago Press, 1990), *The Chain* (University of Chicago Press, 1996*), The Dreamhouse* (University of Chicago Press, 1999), *Far Side of the Earth (*Houghton Mifflin, 2003*),* and a translation of Euripides' *Herakles* (Oxford University Press, 2001). He has won the Shelley Prize from the Poetry Society of America, and grants from the Lila Wallace Fund, the American Academy of Arts and Letters, the Guggenheim Foundation, and the National Endowment for the Arts. He teaches in the MFA program at Hunter College. His new book, *Orders of Daylight,* is forthcoming from Houghton Mifflin Harcourt in fall of 2010.

Of "At the Pool," Sleigh writes: "If you're a committed swimmer, one day you'll find yourself swimming long distances in open water— one of my favorite swims takes me from the lighthouse at Long Point clear across the bay of Provincetown harbor, about a mile and a half. Most times, though, I swim in public pools where light scattering across the pool bottom and the way the acoustics distort sound can give the pool an otherworldly quality—not quite an underworld, but like one. I remember meeting an older friend by accident in the pool and thinking how odd our bodies looked, buoyant and heavy at the same time.

"And so in the poem the contrasts between large and small, between heavy and light, reveal the older man's body through shifts in scale. And the younger man, who hasn't yet learned that being old is as new to the old as being young is to the young, tries to comprehend the older man's loss—and discovers that loss is serial, not final: Eurydice glides away from Orpheus only when he turns to look at her, but comes speeding toward him just as soon as he turns away. The long lines and the way they break down the page are in flux, too; the syntax can't resolve into certainty. At the bottom of the pool is time and the end of time: and on the surface is the way time seems to stretch out and out, even as it's coming to an end."

VINCENT STANLEY was born in Burbank, California, in 1952. He has worked most of his adult life for Patagonia, the outdoor clothing company, for many years as sales manager and more recently as a part-time senior editor for its catalogs. He lives with his wife, the novelist and memoirist Nora Gallagher, in Santa Barbara and in New York. Stanley is at work now on a cycle of poems on wildness as well as on a novel, the third in a quartet, about two American families of the last century.

Of "At the New York Public Library, I heard Derek Walcott dismiss the prose poem," Stanley writes: "It started, in response to Walcott, as play on the sentence versus the line as a poem's formal basis—and on the *use* of a poem, if its language is grief and we live at the heart of an empire. I had also just seen Agnes Martin's wonderful drawings of dots and fine, almost self-erasing lines that run ragged to the edge of the paper. I started to play with the parallels—and struggle with the blind spots. A poem that defends the sentence begins, once under sail, to lean into its lines."

PAMELA SUTTON was born in Ypsilanti, Michigan, in 1960. She holds an MS in journalism from Northwestern University and an MA in creative writing from Boston University, where she was awarded the George Starbuck Fellowship. She taught writing at the University of Pennsylvania for seven years. At present she lives on Marco Island, Florida, which she calls "the land of Hemingway."

Of "Forty," Sutton writes: "Not long after I wrote that poem, I left my job as an editor for Lippincott, said to be America's oldest publishing company, and began teaching writing at the University of Pennsylvania. I entitled my first class 'Writing as Journey.' It was an unconscious choice that the book to which all the other books in that class were hinged was Elie Wiesel's *Night.* As the years and semesters passed, that book became increasingly difficult to teach even as it grew in importance. I write this as an unorthodox Christian at heart: if anyone ever rose from the dead, physically, spiritually, and psychologically, it was Elie Wiesel. If we're looking for heroes in a disturbing cycle of history, look no farther than Elie Wiesel. I never attended one of his lectures while I was a graduate student at Boston University because I was not ready to confront the Holocaust. I was not Jewish, though I absorbed an enormous love of Judaism, having lived in the Netherlands in my twenties. I lived just down the street from the Portuguese Synagogue on Jodensbreestraat, and visited often, always knocked flat by its beauty. And emptiness. Also, as I spelunked into the depths of European history I could only conclude that the Jews shaped Europe into an intellectual and economic powerhouse, and Europe killed them for it. It was a thought I filed away for twenty years until 9/11.

"I became a very different person that day: my English, Irish, and American Indian ancestors rose to the surface and stayed. On an invisible dimension of time, someone plunged a spear through my back, hurling me off my horse, where I landed on the muddy shore of Manhattan. I pulled the spear out of my back, closed my eyes, and drew my bloody fingers down my face, then opened my eyes to a changed world. I am newly dead and newly alive as I attempt to protect my child from Neo-anti-Semitism, while simultaneously teaching her to rejoice in her heritage. She is half Jewish. Her father is Jewish. I did not think 9/11 could possibly hurt more until Daniel Pearl uttered the words 'My mother is Jewish' before terrorists severed his noble and beautiful throat.

"Knowing that his wife was Dutch and expecting their first child multiplied the pain. I wish someone would acknowledge that, as a journalist, he was hot on the trail of bin Laden during an administration that had zero intention of catching bin Laden. Clue: He was not in Iraq.

"I wrote the poem from the steps of Independence Square Park in Philadelphia. And I wrote it almost unconsciously, and in a visceral state of rage. Numbers infuriate me: they can be boring and random, or they can alter history. Like all good journalists, I checked the facts: there are exactly 123 trees in Independence Square Park. There are 260 colors in the hundred thousand glass fragments that make up the Parrish-Tiffany mosaic—a hypnotizing mosaic, which is emblematic of the vision quest that transforms the meaning of numbers in the poem. Pointillist details of nature create a hallucinatory state confounding numbers: 'hawk perched on the weathervane'; 'trees, inhaling, exhaling light'; 'carrying my grandmother'; 'weighs exactly the same as my child'; 'One beloved child.' I am carrying both history and the future in my arms.

"I refer to America as Rome because, though flawed, America's government is a descendant of Rome. I equate al-Qaeda with Visigoths, because their actions have been so hideously barbaric. And I point to the Colossus of Rhodes, because our Statue of Liberty was sculpted by Frédéric Auguste Bartholdi to resemble the ancient Greeks' Colossus. That it is a 'Colossus consecrated to the sun' evokes both the sacred and time itself. At the beginning of the poem I am running on a treadmill to pass the time on my lunch hour. At the end of the poem I am desperately running to reverse time."

ALEXANDRA TEAGUE was born in Fort Worth, Texas, in 1974 and grew up in Eureka Springs, Arkansas. She received a BA from Southwest Missouri State University, an MFA from the University of Florida, and was a 2006–2008 Stegner Fellow at Stanford. She currently lives in Oakland and teaches English at City College of San Francisco. Her first book of poems, *Mortal Geography,* is forthcoming from Persea Press in 2010.

Teague writes: "I began 'Heartlines' with a clichéd come-on in a Miami club—imagining what the speaker might hear if she could literally take the man's advice to listen to your heart. The distant childhood landscape that arose surprised me and led me to think about the histories of place and family, but also the seemingly unimportant details, we carry inside us. Years ago, I wanted to write about the French verbs *apprendre* (to learn) and *apprendre par coeur* (to learn by heart/memorize). I'm interested by the idea that memorization involves the heart, rather than, or in addition to, the mind. I've also been looking for—and am very grateful to have found—a use for the seventy-five counties of Arkansas, which I can, truly, still recite in alphabetical order."

CRAIG MORGAN TEICHER was born in White Plains, New York, in 1979. He is a freelance writer and a board member of the National Book Critics Circle. He teaches at several institutions, including Columbia and Pratt. His first book of poems, *Brenda Is in the Room and Other Poems,* was chosen by Paul Hoover for the 2007 Colorado Prize for Poetry and was published by Center for Literary Publishing. BOA Editions will publish a collection of fiction and fables called *Cradle Book* in 2010. He lives in Brooklyn with his wife and son.

Of "Ultimately Justice Directs Them," Teicher writes: "This poem was written in a rather cynical mood in the middle of what many—myself certainly included—consider one of America's darkest times. I hope that by the time you read this it will seem dated and silly, though I have a nasty feeling that poems about willful ignorance surrounding unjust wars will always be timely."

NATASHA TRETHEWEY was born in Gulfport, Mississippi, in 1966. She is the author of three collections of poetry, *Domestic Work* (Graywolf, 2000), *Bellocq's Ophelia* (Graywolf, 2002), and *Native Guard (*Houghton Mifflin, 2006), which won the Pulitzer Prize. She is the recipient of fellowships from the Guggenheim Foundation, the Rockefeller Foundation, the National Endowment for the Arts, and the Radcliffe Institute for Advanced Study. At Emory University she is professor of English and holds the Phillis Wheatley Distinguished Chair in Poetry.

Of "Liturgy," Trethewey writes: "My hometown is Gulfport, Mississippi—one of the towns along the Gulf Coast that was devastated by Hurricane Katrina. Not long after the storm I went back to see it, and to talk to some of the people there. When I wrote the poem, I was thinking about Margaret Walker Alexander's poem 'For My People.' I was also thinking of the idea of *nostos*—a journey home—and the word 'liturgy,' which, in the original Greek, meant a public duty or one's duty to the state."

DEREK WALCOTT was born in 1930 in the town of Castries in Saint Lucia, one of the Windward Islands in the Lesser Antilles. After studying at St. Mary's College in his native island and at the University of the West Indies in Jamaica, Walcott moved in 1953 to Trinidad. In 1959, he founded the Trinidad Theatre Workshop. He won the Nobel Prize for literature in 1992 ("for a poetic oeuvre of great luminosity, sustained by a historical vision, the outcome of a multicultural commitment"). His books of poetry include *Another Life* (1973), *Sea Grapes* (1976), *The Star-*

Apple Kingdom (1979), *The Fortunate Traveler* (1981), *Midsummer* (1984), *Collected Poems, 1948–1984* (1986), and *Omeros* (1990), a retelling of Homeric stories in a twentieth-century Caribbean setting. Several of Walcott's plays have been produced in the United States, and his first collection of essays, *What the Twilight Says,* was published by Farrar, Straus & Giroux in 1998. Walcott retired from teaching poetry and drama in the creative writing department at Boston University in 2007. *White Egrets,* a new book of poems, will be published by Farrar, Straus & Giroux in 2010.

JEANNE MURRAY WALKER was born in Parkers Prairie, Minnesota, in 1944. Her poems are collected in seven volumes, including *Coming into History* (Cleveland State University, 1990), *A Deed to the Light* (University of Illinois Press, 2004), and *New Tracks, Night Falling* (Wm. B. Eerdmans, 2009). A Fellow of the University Center for Advanced Studies, she has received the Glenna Luschi *Prairie Schooner* Award, seven Pennsylvania Council on the Arts Awards, a National Endowment for the Arts Fellowship, and a Pew Fellowship in the Arts. Her scripts have been produced in theaters in Boston, Washington, Chicago, throughout the Midwest, and in London. She serves on the editorial boards of *Shenandoah* and *Image.* She is a professor of English at the University of Delaware and a mentor in the Seattle Pacific low-residency MFA program.

Walker writes: "'Holding Action' is the final poem in my most recent book, *New Tracks, Night Falling.* Although I frequently forget the exact circumstances of a first draft, I remember feeling fierce hope as I wrote this poem, hope for the book. The life of a book, any book, is so tenuous. Think how many poems and plays and novels and paintings and sculptures and other works of art have been lost. Consider the fire that burned the library at Alexandria and the ransacking of religious art in the reformation. Think about the pillaging of the museum in Baghdad. And what we don't lose by violence, we sometimes lose by neglect, by the randomness of cultural memory.

"And who knows whether fifty years from now we'll even have books? Remember when we used to play records? They were replaced by tapes, which, in turn, were replaced by CDs and computers and phones.

"What are the chances any particular book will survive?

"Every writer, I suppose, tries to build in some defense against these forces as her book goes into the world. One of the most moving of these, at least to me, is the poem Chaucer placed at the end of *Troilus and Criseyde*. *'Go, litel bok, go,'* he says. Go into the world; don't be envious of other poems, but serve poetry. I wasn't thinking consciously about Chaucer when I wrote 'Holding Action,' but Chaucer surely must have been standing behind me."

RONALD WALLACE was born in Cedar Rapids, Iowa, in 1945 and grew up in St. Louis, Missouri. He is codirector of the creative writing program at the University of Wisconsin in Madison and editor for the University of Wisconsin Press's Brittingham and Felix Pollak Prize Poetry Series. His twelve books include *For a Limited Time Only* (2008) and *Long for this World: New and Selected Poems* (2003), both from the University of Pittsburgh Press. He is married and has two grown daughters and three grandchildren. He divides his time between Madison and a forty-acre farm in Bear Valley, Wisconsin.

Of "No Pegasus," Wallace writes: "About a decade ago it occurred to me that I should write a sonnet a day for a year. I had been suffering through a prolonged dry period and, wondering if I would ever write again, I hoped that the obsessive discipline would help to jump-start my muse. I remembered that T. S. Eliot had turned to sonnets late in his career, as had John Berryman; perhaps I could follow in their footsteps. It was an exhilarating, if exhausting, experience. I wrote more than 400 sonnets that year, 200 of which were eventually published in literary magazines and 100 of which appeared as my book *The Uses of Adversity* (University of Pittsburgh Press, 1998).

"On day 365 of my project I laid down my pen and vowed never to write another sonnet. I thought I might write some longer, free verse poems, perhaps some prose, maybe a novel—forms the great world seemed to value more than the sonnet's prancing song.

"Then, last year, on a plane trip from Madison, Wisconsin, to Siesta Key, Florida, facing another dry period, I found myself sitting, without book or notebook or laptop or other means of escape, next to a gregarious salesman who seemed intent on telling me his life story. In desperation, I indicated I had important work to do, and, on the back of my boarding pass, began to write—something, anything. The boarding pass was just about sonnet-size, and what started as gibberish began to shape itself into 'No Pegasus.' Once again the sonnet, that good horse, had come to my rescue and carried me away with it, singing."

CHARLES HARPER WEBB was born in Philadelphia in 1952 and grew up in Houston, Texas. His book of prose poems, *Hot Popsicles*, was published by University of Wisconsin Press in 2005, and his fifth book of verse, *Amplified Dog,* by Red Hen Press in 2006. *Shadow Ball: New & Selected Poems* is forthcoming from University of Pittsburgh Press. He has received the Morse, Pollock, and Saltman prizes, the Kate Tufts Discovery Award, a Whiting Writer's Award, and a Guggenheim Fellowship. A former rock singer, guitarist, and psychotherapist, he has edited *Stand Up Poetry: An Expanded Anthology,* and directs the creative writing program at California State University, Long Beach.

Webb writes: "'Her Last Conflagration' began, I dimly recall, in response to the phrase 'She's hot.' The poem draws, too, on my experience of the wildfires that hit Southern California every fall. I tried to let each line spark the next in a spirit of serious play. Once the imagery caught fire, so to speak, I just stood back and let the language run its course. As to whether, or in what ways, the speaker's experiences with Veronica are reality based, my lips are sealed."

LISA WILLIAMS was born in Nashville, Tennessee, in 1966. Her first book, *The Hammered Dulcimer* (Utah State University Press, 1998), won the May Swenson Poetry Award, and her second book, *Woman Reading to the Sea* (W. W. Norton, 2008), won the Barnard Women Poets Prize. She was awarded the Rome Prize in literature by the American Academy of Arts and Letters in 2004. She teaches literature and creative writing at Centre College in Kentucky.

Of "Leaving Saint Peter's Basilica," Williams writes: "During my year as a Rome Fellow, I visited Saint Peter's numerous times, but one of the best was a visit in February, when I went alone and there was less fanfare in and around the church. I lost myself in the shifting bodies, shadows, and flat winter light as I passed through, and the contrast of those frozen, dramatically gesturing sculptures, so immobile (ostensibly immortal) inside the cavernous church, and the clusters of people moving past, like waves of history, really struck me. I was also feeling the problematic nature of my enterprise—going into these places, writing about them. I felt sheepish and cowed. I sat on one of the benches and tried to jot down, very quickly, some of the impressions that flooded me, but also hiding what I was doing for some reason—I don't know why. No one was watching. I had to go outside before the church closed (that was a favorite time to visit them) and dusk was falling, a winter sunset with pinkish tones around the dome, cross, and sculptures on the roof. It's a gusty, impressionistic poem with a little confession, maybe the best I could hope for in such a place."

CAROLYNE WRIGHT was born in Bellingham, Washington, in 1949, grew up in Seattle, and graduated from Seattle University's Humanities Honors Program. After a year on a Fulbright grant in Chile during the presidency of Salvador Allende, she received her master's and doctorate in English and creative writing from Syracuse University, studying with Philip Booth, George P. Elliott, and W. D. Snodgrass, and briefly with Raymond Carver. She studied with Elizabeth Bishop at the University of Washington and at writers' conferences with Donald Justice, William Stafford, Madeline DeFrees, and Richard Hugo. Her eight books and chapbooks of poetry include *Seasons of Mangoes and Brainfire* (Eastern Washington University Press/Lynx House Books, 2nd ed., 2005); four volumes of poetry in translation from Spanish and Bengali; and a collection of essays. Her most recent collection, *A Change of Maps* (Lost Horse Press, 2006), won the 2007 Independent Book Publishers Bronze Award for Poetry. She spent four years on Indo-U.S. Sub-Commission and Fulbright Senior Research fellowships in Kolkata, India, and Dhaka, Bangladesh, collecting and translating the work of Bengali women poets and writers. After a trip to Chile last fall, she worked on her investigative and literary memoir, *The Road to Isla Negra*. Wright lives in Seattle and teaches in the Whidbey Writers Workshop MFA Program and at Seattle's Richard Hugo House. She served on the board of the Association of Writers and Writing Programs (AWP) from 2004 to 2008.

Of "'This dream the world is having about itself . . .'" Wright says: "Early one morning toward the end of the last millennium, I awakened from a vivid dream in which I was walking across a prairie landscape in golden afternoon light. A line from a William Stafford poem ('This dream the world is having about itself') was echoing in my head, though I didn't recall which poem it was from. (It turned out to be the first line of 'Vocation,' from Stafford's early book *Traveling Through the Dark*.) Bolting awake, I wrote down the line, then others that crowded in afterward—full of storm clouds, high winds, and dry plains sloping toward the blue silhouettes of mountain ranges on the horizon: a terrain familiar from the Inland Northwest plateaus of my native Washington state. There were also images from childhood: the Columbus Day windstorm during the 1962 Seattle World's Fair, photos of my mother and her mother in those flowered dresses from the 1940s, memories of my father watering the front yard with a hose before the advent of lawn sprinklers.

"I scribbled a couple of pages before my feet hit the floor that morning, but I did nothing more until several months later, when I began to fashion a poem from this seemingly random trove of images. The generating line from Bill Stafford's poem insisted in its quiet, not-quite-prose way that it had to remain as the opening. But the lines that followed did not gain rhetorical momentum until I found myself writing 'That summer in our late teens we / walked all evening through town.' Here, the plural 'we' coalesced into an imagined recollection of two sisters walking through a prairie town. Once the older sister's fear of dying in her twenties emerged a few lines later, I began to follow the patterning that suggested itself—of advancing each movement in the poem by a decade, so that the oblique narrative would unfold according to the next decade in sequence. The trope that emerges to direct the poem's progression is of the speaker and her sister walking, decade by decade, through the small Western town of childhood—a setting that seems to haunt my imagination.

"As I wrote, I didn't consciously reference 'Vocation,' but I noticed how echoes from the Stafford poem arose—as elements from a sort of shared inner landscape of origins? Or else I had internalized more of Stafford's world than I knew. This poem is only indirectly autobi-ographical—I never walked anywhere with my older sister, who had suffered severe trauma at birth and lived in an institution almost all her life. But her presence-in-absence resonated throughout my childhood, and the reality of her life and death (in the final weeks of the previous century) has had a persistent influence."

DEBBIE YEE was born in Sacramento, California, in 1973. She lives in San Francisco, where she is an in-house legal counsel for a national bank. She received her undergraduate and law degrees from the University of California at Berkeley, and is a Kundiman fellow (Asian American poetry).

Yee writes: "When I wrote 'Cinderella's Last Will & Testament,' I had just started a job as an associate at a law firm, where I was handed a case for the probate of a decedent who went by the same name as the fictional character. I was struck by the idea that there was tangible evidence—actual court pleadings—that showed that the story of Cin-derella didn't end happily in an enchanted kingdom in the days of yore, but in a gritty, urban city in the twenty-first century where she actu-ally became old and suffered a real death. I started writing about other events that may have occurred during Mrs. Charming's life, and after her death, had she lived as we do. Then I wondered just what happened to all of her stuff."

Kevin Young was born in Lincoln, Nebraska, in 1970 but left before he was one and hasn't made it back. He did root for the Cornhuskers for much of his childhood. His first book, *Most Way Home* (William Morrow, 1995), won the National Poetry Series and the Zacharis First Book Award from *Ploughshares;* his third book, *Jelly Roll: A Blues* (Knopf, 2003), won the Paterson Poetry Prize; his most recent book is *Dear Darkness* (Knopf, 2008). He is currently completing *The Art of Losing: Poems of Grief and Recovery,* an anthology of contemporary elegies (Bloomsbury USA, 2009).

Young writes: "'I shall be released' appears in my latest book, *Dear Darkness,* where it inaugurates a small sequence of poems invoking American places and song. It's an elegy not just to a person, but to language, I suppose, written in one of those cold Indiana winters where you freeze on the way to your mailbox: good writing weather, you could say. Besides being a song, the title is both a wish and a promise."

Matthew Zapruder was born in Washington, D.C., in 1967. He is the author of two collections of poetry: *American Linden* (Tupelo Press, 2002) and *The Pajamaist* (Copper Canyon, 2006). *The Pajamaist* was selected by Tony Hoagland as the winner of the William Carlos Williams Award from the Poetry Society of America. In collaboration with historian Radu Ioanid, Zapruder translated *Secret Weapon: Selected Late Poems of Eugen Jebeleanu* (Coffee House Press, 2007). German and Slovenian language editions of his poems are forthcoming in 2009 from Luxbooks and Serpa Editions; Luxbooks is also publishing a separate German-language graphic novel version of the poem "The Pajamaist." In fall 2007 he was a Lannan Literary Fellow in Marfa, Texas, and he was a recipient in 2008 of a May Sarton prize from the American Academy of Arts and Sciences. His collaborative book with painter Chris Uphues, *For You in Full Bloom,* will be published by Pilot Press in 2009, and his third full-length collection of poems, *Come On All You Ghosts,* is forthcoming from Copper Canyon in 2010. He lives in San Francisco, teaches poetry as a member of the permanent faculty of the Juniper Summer Writing Institute at the University of Massachusetts in Amherst, works as an editor for Wave Books, and teaches in the low-residency MFA program at University of California, Riverside–Palm Desert.

Of "Never to Return," Zapruder writes: "In spring 2005 I was living outside of Los Angeles, spending a lot of my time in the car. One time when I was driving through the city at night I heard someone on the radio say, 'Soon doctors will be able to transplant faces.' I had no idea what that meant, for a second I thought switch them, which seemed interesting and totally pointless. I had recently discovered the 'memo' function on my cell phone, and deciding at that moment on a great new plan to use the time in my car to write poems, I pressed the button and spoke that phrase into the tiny microphone. Then I forgot about it. Many months later while trying to make a call I accidentally turned on that memo function and heard a robot version of my voice saying that phrase. This was a scary and exciting moment. I included it in the poem, along with many other phenomena, real and imagined: how the skyscrapers in Vancouver, B.C., looked from a hotel room window in early evening in January, various facts I had heard somewhere along the way about the catastrophic effects of the introduction of nonnative species to new environments, phrases from bird books, other made-up details from books I have not read and which do not exist, a dead wasp on a windowsill in the room where I was writing, etc. Other moments I tried to include in the poem for some reason didn't fit, or fit all too well, which slowed down the momentum of the poem, who can say exactly why? It felt good to bring many various things in, including the memory about my dyed hair, which is true. It's as if all these things started to fall into place, for some reason I could not exactly articulate, in what Wallace Stevens called 'the obscurity of an order, a whole, a knowledge.' The desire to articulate what seems just out of reach is the engine that drives me and, I hope, the reader, through the poem."

AGNI, poetry eds. Lynne Potts and Jay Deshpande. Boston University, 236 Bay State Road, Boston, MA 02215.

Alaska Quarterly Review, ed. Ronald Spatz. University of Alaska Anchorage, 3211 Providence Drive, Anchorage, AK 99508.

American Literary Review, poetry eds. Bruce Bond and Corey Marks. P.O. Box 311307, University of North Texas, Denton, TX 76203–1307.

American Poetry Review, eds. Stephen Berg, David Bonanno, and Elizabeth Scanlon. 1700 Sansom Street, Suite 800, Philadelphia, PA 19103.

The American Scholar, poetry ed. Langdon Hammer. 1606 New Hampshire Avenue NW, Washington, D.C. 20009.

Antioch Review, poetry ed. Judith Hall. P.O. Box 148, Yellow Springs, OH 45387.

Asheville Poetry Review, managing ed. Keith Flynn. P.O. Box 7086, Asheville, NC 28802.

Barrow Street, eds. Lorna Blake, Patricia Carlin, Peter Covino, and Melissa Hotchkiss. P.O. Box 1831, New York, NY 10156.

Callaloo, ed. Charles H. Rowell. Department of English, Texas A&M University, 4212 TAMU, College Station, TX 77843–4212.

CALYX, senior ed. Beverly McFarland. P.O. Box B, Corvallis, OR 97339.

Cimarron Review, poetry eds. Lisa Lewis, Ai, Alfred Corn. 205 Morrill Hall, English Department, Oklahoma State University, Stillwater, OK 74078.

The Cincinnati Review, poetry ed. Don Bogen. P.O. Box 210069, Cincinnati, OH 45221–0069.

Fence, poetry eds. Caroline Crumpacker, Katy Lederer, Charles Valle, Max Winter. Science Library 320, University at Albany, 1400 Washington Avenue, Albany, NY 12222.

FIELD, eds. David Young and David Walker. Oberlin College Press, 50 N. Professor St., Oberlin, OH 44074.

Five Points, eds. David Bottoms and Megan Sexton. P.O. Box 3999, Atlanta, GA 30302–3999.

Fulcrum, eds. Philip Nikolayev and Katia Kapovich. 421 Huron Avenue, Cambridge, MA 02138.

The Georgia Review, ed. Stephen Corey. The University of Georgia, Athens, GA 30602–9009.

The Gettysburg Review, ed. Peter Stitt. Gettysburg College, Gettysburg, PA 17325–1491.

Harper's, ed. Roger D. Hodge. 666 Broadway, New York, NY 10012. www.harpers.org.

The Hudson Review, ed. Paula Dietz. 684 Park Avenue, New York, NY 10021.

Image, ed. Gregory Wolfe. 3307 Third Avenue West, Seattle, WA 98119.

Indiana Review, poetry ed. Ryan Teitman. Ballantine Hall 465, Indiana University, Bloomington, IN 47405–7103.

The Iowa Review, ed. David Hamilton. 308 EPB, The University of Iowa, Iowa City, IA 52242.

Jacket, ed. John Tranter. jacketmagazine.com.

The Journal, poetry ed. Kathy Fagan. Department of English, The Ohio State University, 164 West 17th Avenue, Columbus, OH 43210.

The Kenyon Review, poetry ed. David Baker. www.kenyonreview.org.

La Petite Zine, editors-in-chief Jeffrey Salane and Danielle Pafunda. www.lapetitezine.org.

London Review of Books, ed. Mary-Kay Wilmers. 28 Little Russell Street, London WC1A 2HN.

Margie: The American Journal of Poetry, Robert Nazarene, editor-&-chief and James B. Wilson, senior editor. P.O. Box 250, Chesterfield, MO 63006–0250.

Measure, eds. Paul Bone and Rob Griffith. Department of English, University of Evansville, 1800 Lincoln Avenue, Evansville, IN 47722.

Mid-American Review, poetry ed. Karen Craigo. Box W, Department of English, BGSU, Bowling Green, OH 43403.

The Missouri Review, poetry ed. Katy Didden. 357 McReynolds Hall, University of Missouri, Columbia, MO 65211.

The Nation, poetry ed. Peter Gizzi. 33 Irving Place, New York, NY 10003.

The New Criterion, eds. Hilton Kramer and Roger Kimball. 900 Broadway, Suite 602, New York, NY 10003.

New England Review, poetry ed. C. Dale Young. Middlebury College, Middlebury, VT 05753.

The New Republic, poetry ed. C. K. Williams. www.tnr.com.

The New York Quarterly, ed. Raymond Hammond. P.O. Box 2015, Old Chelsea Station, New York, NY 10113.

The New Yorker, poetry ed. Paul Muldoon. 4 Times Square, New York, NY 10036.

No Tell Motel, ed. Reb Livingston. www.notellmotel.org.

OCHO, ed. Didi Menendez. www.mipoesias.com/ocho.

Painted Bride Quarterly, eds. Kathleen Volk Miller and Marion Wrenn. Drexel University, Department of English and Philosophy, 3141 Chestnut Street, Philadelphia, PA 19104.

The Paris Review, poetry eds. Dan Chiasson and Meghan O'Rourke. 62 White Street, New York, NY 10013.

Parnassus: Poetry in Review, ed. Herbert Leibowitz. 205 W. 89th Street, #8F, New York, NY 10024.

Pleiades: A Journal of New Writing, eds. Kevin Prufer and Wayne Miller. Department of English, University of Central Missouri, Warrensburg, MO 64093.

Ploughshares, poetry ed. John Skoyles. Emerson College, 120 Boylston St., Boston, MA 02116–4624.

Poet Lore, eds. Jody Bolz and E. Ethelbert Miller. The Writer's Center, 4508 Walsh Street, Bethesda, MD 20815.

Poetry, ed. Christian Wiman. 444 N. Michigan Avenue, Suite 1850, Chicago, IL 60611–4034.

Prairie Schooner, Editor-in-Chief Hilda Raz. 201 Andrews Hall, P.O. Box 880334, Lincoln, NE 68588–0334.

Provincetown Arts, Christopher Busa, ed. 650 Commercial Street, Provincetown, MA 02657.

Salt Hill, poetry ed. Billy Templeton III. Syracuse University, English Department, Syracuse, NY 13244.

Shenandoah, ed. R. T. Smith. Mattingly House, 2 Lee Avenue, Washington and Lee University, Lexington, VA 24450–2116.

The Southern Review, ed. Jeanne Leiby. Old President's House, LSU, Baton Rouge, LA 70803.

Southwest Review, ed. Willard Spiegelman. Southern Methodist University, P.O. Box 750374, Dallas, TX 75275–0374.

Third Coast, poetry eds. Laura Donnelly and Gary McDowell. Western Michigan University, English Department, 1903 W. Michigan Ave., Kalamazoo, MI 49008–5331.

Vanitas, ed. Vincent Katz. 211 West 19th Street, #5, New York, NY 10011. vanitasmagazine@mac.com. www.vanitasmagazine.net.

The Virginia Quarterly Review, ed. Ted Genoways. One West Range, Box 400223, Charlottesville, VA 22904–4223.

ACKNOWLEDGMENTS

The series editor wishes to thank Mark Bibbins for his invaluable assistance. I am grateful as well to Mary Jo Bang, Jill Baron, Julia Cohen, Bruce Covey, Allison Green, George Green, Stacey Harwood, Jennifer Michael Hecht, Elizabeth Howort, Cole Larsen, Ben Mirov, Honor Moore, Kathleen Ossip, Angela Patrinos, Greg Santos, Michael Schiavo, and Paul Violi. Warm thanks go, as always, to Glen Hartley and Lynn Chu of Writers' Representatives, and to Alexis Gargagliano, my editor, and Jessica Manners, Erich Hobbing, David Stanford Burr, and Daniel Cuddy of Scribner.

Grateful acknowledgment is made of the magazines in which these poems first appeared and the magazine editors who selected them. A sincere attempt has been made to locate all copyright holders. Unless otherwise noted, copyright to the poems is held by the individual poets.

John Ashbery: "They Knew What They Wanted" from *Planisphere* © 2009 by John Ashbery. Reprinted by permission of Ecco/Harper-Collins. The poem also appeared in the *London Review of Books* and *Vanitas*. Reprinted by permission of the poet.

Caleb Barber: "Beasts and Violins" appeared in *Poet Lore*. Reprinted by permission of the poet.

Mark Bibbins: "Concerning the Land to the South of Our Neighbors to the North" from *The Dance of No Hard Feelings*. © 2009 by Mark Bibbins. Reprinted by permission of Copper Canyon Press. Also appeared in *La Petite Zine*.

Bruce Bond: "Ringtone" appeared in *Ploughshares*. Reprinted by permission of the poet.

Marianne Boruch: "The Doctor" from *Grace, Fallen From*. © 2008 by Marianne Boruch. Reprinted by permission of Wesleyan University Press. Also appeared in the *Cincinnati Review*.

Fleda Brown: "Roofers" appeared in the *Georgia Review*. Reprinted by permission of the poet.

Catherine Carter: "The Book of Steve" appeared as "Adam and Steve" in *Asheville Poetry Review*. Reprinted by permission of the poet.

Suzanne Cleary: "From *The Boy's Own Book: A Compleat Encyclopedia of*

All the Diversions Athletic, Scientific, and Recreative, of Boyhood and Youth, by William Clarke" appeared in *Margie*. Reprinted by permission of the poet.

Billy Collins: "The Great American Poem" appeared in the *Virginia Quarterly Review*. Reprinted by permission of the poet.

Rob Cook: "The Song of America" appeared in *Fence*. Reprinted by permission of the poet.

James Cummins: "Freud" appeared in the *Antioch Review*. Reprinted by permission of the poet.

Mark Doty: "Apparition (Favorite Poem)" from *Fire to Fire: New and Selected Poems*. © 2008 by Mark Doty. Reprinted by permission of HarperCollins. Also appeared in *Five Points*.

Denise Duhamel: "How It Will End" appeared in *Barrow Street*. Reprinted by permission of the poet.

Alice Friman: "Getting Serious" appeared in *Ploughshares*. Reprinted by permission of the poet.

Margaret Gibson: "Black Snake" appeared in the *Georgia Review*. Reprinted by permission of the poet.

Douglas Goetsch: "First Time Reading Freud" from *The Job of Being Everybody*. © 2003 by Douglas Goetsch. Reprinted by permission of Cleveland State University Press. Also appeared in the *New York Quarterly*.

Albert Goldbarth: "Zones" from *To Be Read in 500 Years*. © 2009 by Albert Goldbarth. Reprinted by permission of Graywolf Press. Also appeared in *Shenandoah*.

Barbara Goldberg: "The Fullness Thereof" appeared in the *Gettysburg Review*. Reprinted by permission of the poet.

Michael J. Grabell: "Definition of Terms" appeared in *Southwest Review*. Reprinted by permission of the poet.

Debora Greger: "Eve in the Fall" appeared in the *New Criterion*. Reprinted by permission of the poet.

Jennifer Grotz: "The Record" appeared in the *Southern Review*. Reprinted by permission of the poet.

Barbara Hamby: "Ode to Airheads, Hairdos, Trains to and from Paris" from *All-Night Lingo Tango*. © 2009 by Barbara Hamby. Reprinted by permission of the University of Pittsburgh Press. Also appeared in *Indiana Review*.

Sarah Hannah: "The Safe House" from *Inflorescence* (Tupelo Press, 2007). © The Estate of Sarah Hannah. Used by permission. Also appeared in *Painted Bride Quarterly*.

Jerry Harp: "Houses" appeared in *Pleiades*. Reprinted by permission of the poet.

Jim Harrison: "Sunday Discordancies" appeared in *Five Points*. Reprinted by permission of the poet.

Dolores Hayden: "Grave Goods" appeared in *Southwest Review*. Reprinted by permission of the poet.

Terrance Hayes: "A House Is Not a Home" appeared in *Callaloo*. Reprinted by permission of the poet.

K. A. Hays: "The Way of All the Earth" from *Dear Apocalypse*. © 2009 by K. A. Hays. Reprinted by permission of Carnegie Mellon University Press. Also appeared in the *Antioch Review*.

Bob Hicok: "Mum's the word" appeared in the *Georgia Review*. Reprinted by permission of the poet.

Daniel Hoffman: "A Democratic Vista" appeared in the *New Criterion*. Reprinted by permission of the poet.

Richard Howard: "Arthur Englander's Back in School" from *Without Saying* (Turtle Point Press, 2008). © 2008 by Richard Howard. Reprinted by permission. Also appeared in *The New Republic*.

P. Hurshell: "In Winter" appeared in *CALYX*. Reprinted by permission of the poet.

Michael Johnson: "How to Be Eaten by a Lion" appeared in *Mid-American Review*. Reprinted by permission of the poet.

Tina Kelley: "To Yahweh" appeared in *Southwest Review*. Reprinted by permission of the poet.

Maud Kelly: "What I Think of Death, If Anyone's Asking" appeared in *American Literary Review*. Reprinted by permission of the poet.

Lance Larsen: "Why do you keep putting animals in your poems?" appeared in *Indiana Review*. Reprinted by permission of the poet.

Phillis Levin: "Open Field" appeared in the *Kenyon Review*. Reprinted by permission of the poet.

Philip Levine: "Words on the Wind" appeared in the *Georgia Review*. Reprinted by permission of the poet.

Sarah Lindsay: "Tell the Bees" from *Twigs and Knucklebones*. © 2008 by Sarah Lindsay. Reprinted by permission of Copper Canyon Press. Also appeared in *Poetry*.

Thomas Lux: "The Happy Majority" from *God Particles*. © 2008 by Thomas Lux. Reprinted by permission of Houghton Mifflin. Also appeared in *American Poetry Review*.

Joanie Mackowski, "Boarding: *Hemaris thysbe*" from *View from a Temporary Window*. © 2009 by Joanie Mackowski. Reprinted by the

Martha Silano: "Love" appeared in the *Cincinnati Review*. Reprinted by permission of the poet.

Mitch Sisskind: "Like a Monkey" appeared in *Jacket*. Reprinted by permission of the poet.

Tom Sleigh: "At the Pool" appeared in *AGNI*. Reprinted by permission of the poet.

Vincent Stanley: "At the New York Public Library, I heard Derek Walcott dismiss the prose poem." appeared in *Fulcrum*. Reprinted by permission of the poet.

Pamela Sutton: "Forty" appeared in *American Poetry Review*. Reprinted by permission of the poet.

Alexandra Teague: "Heartlines" appeared in *New England Review*. Reprinted by permission of the poet.

Craig Morgan Teicher: "Ultimately Justice Directs Them" appeared in *No Tell Motel*. Reprinted by permission of the poet.

Natasha Trethewey: "Liturgy" appeared in the *Virginia Quarterly Review*. Reprinted by permission of the poet.

Derek Walcott: "A Sea-Change" from *White Egrets*. © 2009 by Derek Walcott. Reprinted by permission of Farrar, Straus & Giroux. Also appeared in *AGNI* and *Harper's*.

Jeanne Murray Walker: "Holding Action" from *New Tracks, Night Falling* (Eerdmans, 2009) © 2009 by Jeanne Murray Walker. Reprinted by permission. Also appeared in the *Hudson Review*.

Ronald Wallace: "No Pegasus" from *For a Limited Time Only*. © 2008 by Ronald Wallace. Reprinted by permission of The University of Pittsburgh Press. Also appeared in *Margie*.

Charles Harper Webb: "Her Last Conflagration" appeared in *Salt Hill*. Reprinted by permission of the poet.

Lisa Williams: "Leaving Saint Peter's Basilica" from *Woman Reading to the Sea*. © 2008 by Lisa Williams. Reprinted by permission of W. W. Norton & Co. Also appeared in *Measure*.

Carolyne Wright: "'This dream the world is having about itself . . .'" appeared in the *Iowa Review*. Reprinted by permission of the poet.

Debbie Yee: "Cinderella's Last Will & Testament" appeared in *OCHO*. Reprinted by permission of the poet.

Kevin Young: "I shall be released" from *Dear Darkness*. © 2008 by Kevin Young. Reprinted by permission of Alfred A. Knopf, Inc. Also appeared in the *Kenyon Review*.

Matthew Zapruder: "Never to Return" appeared in the *Paris Review*. Reprinted by permission of the poet.